THE Disney PARTY HANDBOOK

THE Disney PARTY HANDBOOK

BY ALISON BOTELER

Disney PRESS

NEW YORK

My special thanks to . . .

Jackee Mason, for her invaluable assistance.
Mary Beth Mueller, for inspiring this project.
Julia Child, for being my mentor.

Last but not least, Mom, Dad, and Disney, for filling my childhood
with imagination.

Photography: Ed Freeman, White Light, Inc.
Prop styling: Charla Boteler
Food styling: Alison Boteler

First Edition
1 3 5 7 9 10 8 6 4 2

Library of Congress Cataloging-in-Publication Data
Boteler, Alison Molinare.
The Disney party handbook / Alison Boteler.
p. cm.
ISBN 1-56282-173-3 (trade) — ISBN 1-56282-200-4 (lib. bdg.)
1. Children's parties — Handbooks, manuals, etc. 2. Animated
films. 3. Walt Disney Productions. I. Title.
GV1205.B63 1992 793.2′1 — dc20 91-58610 CIP

C O N T E N T S

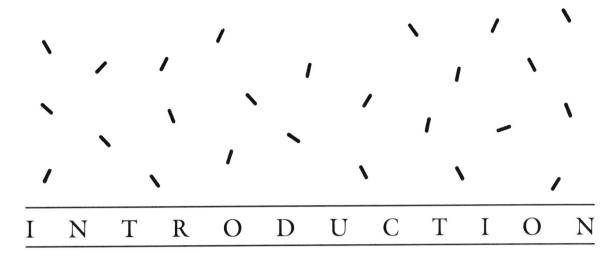

INTRODUCTION

My first birthday memory is of a Dumbo circus party my mother threw for me in our backyard. I awoke that morning to a four year old's fantasy day. It started with ice cream for breakfast (highly recommended . . . once a year)! But I was too excited to eat even one bite. Outside the kitchen window I could see a pink-and-white striped tent made of bed sheets. Calliope music rang out from a record player, and streamers and balloons fluttered in the breeze. Even my dog had a clown ruff around her neck. On the kitchen table was a box, beautifully wrapped in shiny polka-dot paper. It was my first present of the day—a satiny costume with a big, blue plastic elephant head. It was Dumbo.

I remember admiring myself in the mirror moments before my guests arrived. I was Dumbo! I think all my friends gave me Hula Hoops for gifts, because we ended up playing "ringmaster" and jumping through hoops like animals in a circus act. The crowning glory of the day was the cake Mom baked. It was a pink elephant filled with Maraschino cherries. No dessert will ever taste as delicious to me as that cake did on that day.

That summer was the twentieth-anniversary rerelease of the classic Walt Disney film. My mother took me to see the movie, the same one that had been *her* first movie when *she* was a child. *Dumbo* and the birthday party I had that year became childhood memories that will last me a lifetime. Disney's beloved characters can help you turn your child's next birthday party into an unforgettable event, full of delight, laughter, and memories to share in the years ahead.

Choosing a Theme

Obviously, your child's age and interests should be key factors in choosing a Disney party theme. Disney's films appeal to a broad range of ages, and so can Disney theme parties. Children will appreciate different elements of a party at different levels of maturity (until they finally outgrow them). The food, games, and activities detailed for each party in this book are merely suggestions to help you get started. As a parent, you should select the elements of any party that are most appropriate for your child's peer group.

Not only do children's interests change as they grow, but so do their party needs. Below is a list of some basics—divided into age categories—to bear in mind when planning a party.

Each party in this book includes a suggested age range that may span two of the categories on page viii. Use the age ranges as a guide to help you select the right theme party.

Ages 1 to 3: These first parties are a package deal—a parent should accompany each child. A child this age needs a parent around to keep him or her calm and happy. This type of party is also a wonderful opportunity for families to socialize and compare child-rearing notes. Your party preparation efforts are actually more for the parent's pleasure than for the child's. Just remember that toddler parties should always be visually exciting and based on simple concepts. The Dumbo Party, the Winnie the Pooh Party, and the 101 Dalmatians Puppy Party in this book can all be easily adapted for this age-group.

Ages 4 to 6: By now, the birthday-party concept has really begun to sink in. Children of this age are an enthusiastic audience, ready to be entertained. Keep games short and simple; too many activities will wear kids out. This age-group tires quickly.

Ages 7 to 9: This is the prime time, agewise, for parties. Children become active in the planning and preparation of their own parties. Energy levels are high, so games and activities must live up to the challenge.

Ages 10 to 12: This age-group takes the most effort to impress. Movies and swimming or skating parties are popular, and girls of this age enjoy slumber parties.

How Large? How Long?

After years of experience in this department, I've concluded that one dozen guests should be the maximum party size. There are still enough children to play games and create that special aura of party excitement—without too much chaos. You should have *at least* one extra adult for every three children to help keep things under control. Six children, six parents is a good size for preschool parties.

Unfortunately, planning a party's size isn't always a matter of applying a simple formula. Frequently, a child feels obliged to invite his or her entire class to avoid hurt feelings. Also, children may have collected "party payback" obligations throughout the year. When a large party is inevitable, don't panic. Enlist the aid of additional adults and make any necessary changes to the original party plan. Limit the menu. Don't feel obligated to serve a full-course meal. For a large group, just concentrate on the cake and ice cream (doubling recipes as needed).

For very young children, keep the party *short* (about 1¼ to 1½ hours). For older children, and when you serve a complete menu, you'll want to have a full-length party (about 2½ hours). For an extralarge party with a limited menu (cake and ice cream), you can shorten the party to 1½ hours. Remember to figure in drop-off and pick-up time. Children don't all arrive or leave on schedule.

Invitations

A creative party deserves a creative invitation. It's simple to buy them at a stationery store . . . but so much more fun to design your own. If your child is old enough to write, he or she can help make invitations—and get involved in the whole party-planning process.

Homemade invitations are often oversized, so check your local office-supply store for large envelopes of various dimensions. Be sure to mail (or hand deliver) invitations about two to three weeks before the date of the party. Any earlier than that, parents may forget the date; any later, families may have made other plans. It's a good idea to write "RSVP" on the invitation. That way, you're more likely to hear from everyone than if you simply write "Regrets Only." People tend to forget to "regret"; no response does not necessarily mean someone is going to attend. If you're not sure of the party size, the planning process and food preparation can turn into a guessing game.

Competing Parties

Conflicting parties are unavoidable. Everyone seems to want to celebrate his or her birthday on a Saturday afternoon.

Never allow another party on the same day to become an opportunity for a popularity contest. As soon as another party comes to your attention, phone the other child's parents and try to reach a compromise. If necessary, offer to reschedule your child's party. If this isn't an option, offer to coordinate the parties so that one is in the morning and one is in the afternoon. You might even suggest combining the parties into a double celebration at one location. Some parents will actually be eager to split the labor and expense.

Get-acquainted Activity

It's noon. Five children have arrived, seven more are on the way. What do you do to keep the first arrivals occupied? How do you discourage them from disturbing the food and decorations before the rest of the guests can see them? How do you break the ice and encourage interaction? I consider these first few minutes to be a critical part of any party—they can set the tone for the whole party. As soon as the kids *start* to have a good time, they'll continue to have a good time. That's why I've included a get-acquainted activity for every party in this book. The activity is usually something simple: a craft, costume, or exercise that introduces the guests to the party's theme. It should be something each child can work on either independently or with a small group. This will allow arriving guests to join in without interrupting any "work in progress."

Fantasy Feature

A hat, a favor, or any special treat that each guest takes home as a souvenir can be the fantasy feature of a party. The fantasy feature can also be a key element in the party table decor, such as Ariel's Treasure Chest in the Little Mermaid Party. Whenever you're short on preparation time, consider having the fantasy feature be the get-acquainted activity.

Games

Many of the party games in this book have familiar rules, but what makes them different is their connection to classic Disney movies. By encouraging children to identify with their favorite characters, these games are a fun way to extend the fantasy of the films. Each party has two or three suggested games or activities. And remember, when it comes to party games, "rules are meant to be broken." I've seen circumstances where, as a game is played, it evolves into something else entirely. As long as the children are having fun, there's no need to be rigid about rules. After all, the whole point of a party is to have fun!

Expect there to be a poor winner, a poor loser, or even a child who, for whatever reason, is unable to have fun. A child's personality traits are often magnified in party settings, and you should always deal with the children tactfully. When a problem personality surfaces, it's not your role to try to change the child or play psychologist. Just help the child adapt as well as possible to the party experience.

Prizes

Prizes are an essential part of parties and should always be small, simple, inexpensive objects or treats. (The fact that one "wins" them makes them special!) Try wrapping prizes in colored tissue paper to create some suspense. Some suggestions are small boxes of crayons, markers, paint kits, combs or brushes, mirrors, whistles, plastic jewelry, bubble pipes, yo-yos, bandannas, bright socks, magnets, rubber balls, pin-ball puzzles, miniature cars, planes, or animals. Interesting lollipops, chocolate coins, unusual candies, or popcorn balls make good edible prizes. For a nutritious twist, try wrapping apples and oranges in colored plastic wrap with ribbons.

You might not find it necessary to award prizes for every game. There will be some games that have no definitive ending and, therefore, no clear winner. For other games, however, you'll want to award prizes to an entire team.

Party Food

All of the recipes in this book, unless otherwise noted, are based on yielding twelve servings. For smaller parties, most of the recipes may be cut in half. Specialty cakes, however, are the exception. You can't, after all, bake half a Crocodile Cake or half of Davy Crockett's Cocoa Log Cabin Cake. Besides, even with a smaller party, leftover cake is a rare commodity! Remember that although complete menus are given for each party, they are only meant as suggestions. You should not feel as if you must make everything. You may want to serve only dessert (as is traditionally done with large parties). If your child *hates* something on a particular party menu and insists on a favorite food, of course that's what you should serve.

Most children are finicky when it comes to food. However, they may be more adventurous away from home. A party is a wonderful place to introduce young palates to new taste sensations. Oversized food, undersized food, and finger food all fascinate children and may entice them to try something new.

Planning when to prepare the food is important, particularly if you don't have a lot of spare time. There's no need to leave everything for the last minute. If you set aside a few evenings before the party, you can make and freeze a lot of the foods. Preparation times, baking times, and chilling and/or freezing times have been provided for each recipe in the book. Before you make *any* frozen dessert, always measure your freezer! There's nothing more frustrating than creating an edible work of art, then watching it melt because it won't fit in the freezer. Getting the food ready for a party should be a pleasant experience, one to share with your child as much as possible.

A note about toothpicks: They're essential for holding certain party foods together. (Pieces of dried spaghetti can also work well when anchoring soft foods.) Always be sure to tell children about any inedible objects in the food.

Nutrition Note

There's a growing concern among many parents about the amounts of sugar, fat, and cholesterol in their children's diets. Generally, sugar-free beverages can be used in drink recipes. Margarine may be used in place of butter. Nonfat mayonnaise may replace regular mayonnaise in salads. Reduced-fat cheeses can be used instead of richer varieties. Yogurt can often substitute for sour cream. Even ground turkey can take the place of ground beef in many recipes.

Cakes, however, are a precise science. Omissions of sugar or substituting margarine for butter will result in disaster! You can always replace ice cream with frozen yogurt in frozen desserts . . . but please, don't mess with the cake. To those parents who are resistant, all I can say is—a birthday comes only once a year. Let them eat cake!

Cake Creations

The cake is the climax of a birthday, the pinnacle of the party, the focus of the fantasy theme. What it isn't, or shouldn't be, is intimidating to make. You do not need specialty cake pans to make any of the cakes in this book. An industry has evolved around novelty pans of limited potential (it's a whale one year, a guitar the next). But these are really needless investments. All you need are basic pans: 8 inches, 9 inches, or 10 inches round, 8 or 9 inches square, 9 × 13 inches rectangular, 10-inch tube, and 12-inch bundt. You can create just about any shape imaginable by cutting these cakes and rearranging their pieces into edible sculptures. You can even bake dome-shaped cakes in bowls. This is a fun art form, once you are familiar with it.

Batters and Frostings

Most of the cake recipes in this book are from scratch, using a one-bowl method for mixing convenience. However, if you're pinched for time, do not hesitate to use a cake mix instead. There's nothing wrong with taking a shortcut. In fact, with more complicated cake constructions, I actually recommend using a mix to save time.

Frostings are another matter. The amount of frosting in a typical canned product is just too skimpy to successfully cover a specialty cake. And by the time you prepare a frosting mix, you might as well have made it from scratch. Besides, nothing can compare with the flavor of homemade frosting. The recipes in this book yield an ample supply for cake coverage—it's always better to have a little extra than not quite enough. After all, one of the greatest joys in childhood is to lick the frosting left over in the bowl from your own birthday cake!

To create colored frostings, you should always use paste or gel-type food colorings, available at all cake decorating and gourmet cookware shops. Gel colors are now also in many supermarkets. Liquid food colors lack the vibrant intensities of pastes and gels and will also thin down your frosting.

Sometimes you will only want a very small amount of frosting, in a particular color. You might just want to have a bit of blue sky or a patch of green grass on a cake. Instead of tinting, and therefore wasting an entire batch of icing to achieve this effect, you can do something called color glazing. This is the technique of spreading a small amount of gel food coloring across the surface of a white-frosted cake using the back of a metal spatula.

You want to avoid having frosting smeared around the base of a cake. When you're decorating a cake on a platter (or on a covered board), slip strips of waxed paper underneath the cake, around all of the edges. When the frosting has been smoothly applied, gently "snatch" the papers away, and the excess frosting will be gone.

Another thing to avoid when decorating a cake is "crumble pox," when surface cake crumbs show up in the frosting. To control crumble pox, apply stripes of base frosting with a pastry bag, and gently smooth the stripes together to form a uniform surface.

You will need to purchase several pastry bags, coupling nozzles, and decorating tips to add decorative touches to your cake. Coupling nozzles attach the tips to bags, and the decorating tips allow you to do figure piping. You can add stars, leaves, flowers, and other shapes to a frosted cake for a three-dimensional effect. Here is a list of basic pastry bags and decorating tips to begin collecting. They will come in handy for years to come, and they can be used to decorate other foods as well.

Pastry Bags:	You should look for reusable plastic-coated bags, 12, 16, and 20 inches in length. Disposable bags are convenient for small amounts of frosting.
Round Tips:	#2, #3, #4 (small); #10 or #12 (medium); #5 or #6 (large)
Star Tips:	#18, #21 (small); #5 (medium); #4B, #8B (large)
Leaf Tips:	#66 or #67
Ribbon Tip:	#48

Post-party Depression

The party's over. It may be a relief to you, but it's one of the lowest points in your child's life. A child may have anticipated the party and presents for months in advance. Now it won't happen again for a whole year—and that can seem like an eternity.

To ease the transition from birthday to "unbirthday," plan to set aside an unopened present (one from you or from out-of-town friends or relatives) for a rainy day. Save a piece of cake in the freezer, and surprise your child with it a few weeks after the party. A few occasional birthday "encores" can chase away those post-party blues.

WINNIE THE POOH PARTY

Ages 3 to 6

Winnie the Pooh is the creation of A. A. Milne, an English writer who based many of his memorable characters on his son's collection of stuffed animals. Beginning in 1966, Disney began to use the Pooh stories as the basis for four featurette films. Now Winnie the Pooh is the star of his own Saturday morning cartoon show, along with bouncy Tigger, lovable Piglet, mopey Eeyore, and all the other characters of the Hundred-Acre Wood.

Invitation: Owl Card

Decorations: Picnic Motif—red-checkered tablecloth; Pooh plates; graham cracker bears and honey pots; Christopher Robin kite-tail napkins; Piglet balloons

Get-acquainted Activity: Baby Roo Jelly-bean Bags

Fantasy Feature: Eeyore Ears and Donkey Tails

Games: Tigger Tag, Hide the Honey from the Heffalumps, Roo Toss

Menu: Orange-pineapple Owls; Pooh Bear's Burger Biscuits (with Honey Mustard); Piglet's Pink Potato Salad; Peanut Butter Pooh Cake; Frozen Tiggers; Hundred-Acre Wood Honey Apple Punch.

Owl Card

Pooh's friend Owl asks guests to come to a picnic at Pooh's house, being thrown by all the characters in the Hundred-Acre Wood, in honor of your child's birthday.

Materials
6 9″ × 12″ sheets poster board
ruler
scissors
carbon paper
black felt-tip pen
light brown and yellow felt-tip markers
12 5″ × 7″ envelopes

Directions
Cut the sheets into 9″ × 6″ strips. Fold the strips leaving the crease at the top, and form cards that measure 4½″ × 6″. Transfer the picture of Owl's face onto the front of each card by tracing the pattern on page 3 over a piece of carbon paper placed on each card. Outline each face with a black felt-tip pen. Fill in the area around the eyes with a light brown felt-tip marker. Color the beak yellow. Underneath Owl's face write the following: GUESS WHOO'S HAVING A BIRTHDAY PARTY? On the inside of each invitation write the following:

Owl I know is that Pooh,
Rabbit, Piglet, and I are
planning a picnic for
(your child's name)
Come to the House at Pooh Corner
(your address)
on (date) at (time)
RSVP: (your phone number)
P.S. Don't bring any bees!

OWL INVITATION

Preparation time: 1 hour

GUESS WHOO'S HAVING A BIRTHDAY PARTY?

D E C O R A T I O N S

Even if you're planning to hold this party indoors, it should still seem like a picnic. Start with a red-checkered tablecloth and set the table with Pooh plates. To make them, cut out ears from brown construction paper and staple them onto golden brown paper plates. On each plate draw Pooh's face with nontoxic markers. Fill two small baskets—one for each end of the table—with graham cracker bears and provide little honey pots for dipping them. Use the Peanut Butter Pooh Cake as the table's centerpiece. To make place markers, punch holes in one corner of each paper napkin and knot ribbons through the hole to create the look of kite tails. Then write one child's name on each Christopher Robin kite-tail napkin. Hang Piglet balloons over the table. You can make these by drawing Piglet's face on each balloon and taping two pink construction-paper ears onto each one.

GET - ACQUAINTED ACTIVITY

Baby Roo Jelly-bean Bags

Children fill their own bags with jelly beans that they select themselves. The bags will be used in the Roo Toss game, and afterward, the jelly beans will make for fun snacking.

Materials
12 beige (or brown) boy's socks (light-gauge knit)
4 doz. cotton balls
4 yds. heavy-gauge red yarn
scissors
12 white paper sales tags with holes (available at stationery supply stores)
black felt-tip fabric pen
4 lbs. jelly beans, in assorted flavors

Directions
Put about four cotton balls in the toes of each sock and tie off tightly with the red yarn (fig. 1). Thread the sales tags onto the yarn and tie the yarn in a bow. The tied-off portion of the sock will form Roo's head. Draw baby kangaroo faces on heads with a felt-tip pen and write one child's name on each tag. Set up a table with bowls of jelly beans—each flavor in a separate bowl—and a basket of the baby Roos. As guests arrive, show them to the table and tell them to fill their own personal Roo with their favorite flavors of jelly beans. When the socks are pretty well stuffed, help the children tightly tie the bottoms closed with more red yarn (fig. 2).

Preparation time: 8 minutes per Roo

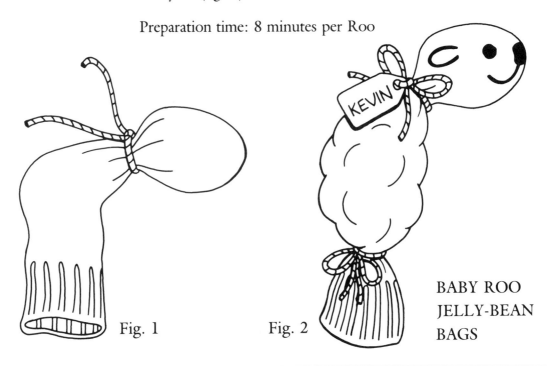

Fig. 1

Fig. 2

BABY ROO JELLY-BEAN BAGS

WINNIE THE POOH PARTY—Orange-pineapple Owl (p. 8), Pooh Bear's Burger Biscuits (p. 8), and Peanut Butter Pooh Cake (p. 12)

Eeyore Ears

Eeyore's floppy donkey ears make fun party hats, and they even come with pin-on tails. (Eeyore is always losing his!)

Materials
2½ yds. gray felt
1 yd. pink felt
tracing paper
1 thin sheet poster board
rubber cement
pencil or tailor's chalk
fabric glue
stapler

Directions
With tracing paper and pencil, trace the ear patterns on page 6. Cut out the tracings and glue them onto a thin sheet of poster board to make stencils. Cut the stencils out and cut 24 outer ears from the gray felt and 24 inner ears from the pink felt. Paste the pink ears to the gray ears with fabric glue. Cut 12 2″-wide and 24″-long strips from the gray felt to make headbands. Using your child's head as a guide, adjust bands to fit and staple in the back. (There should be a 3″ to 4″ overlap.) Fold each ear (fig. 1) and staple to the inside of the headband (fig. 2). The ears should drop over the top of the headband, and the pink ears should face forward.

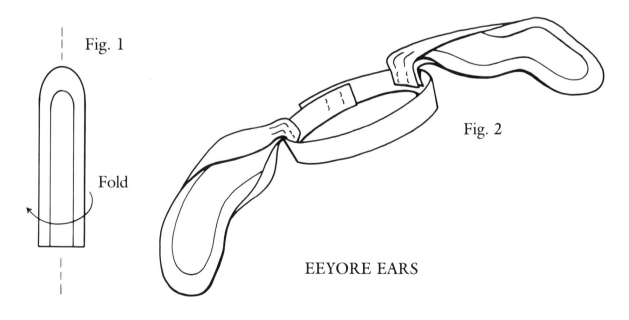

Fig. 1

Fold

Fig. 2

EEYORE EARS

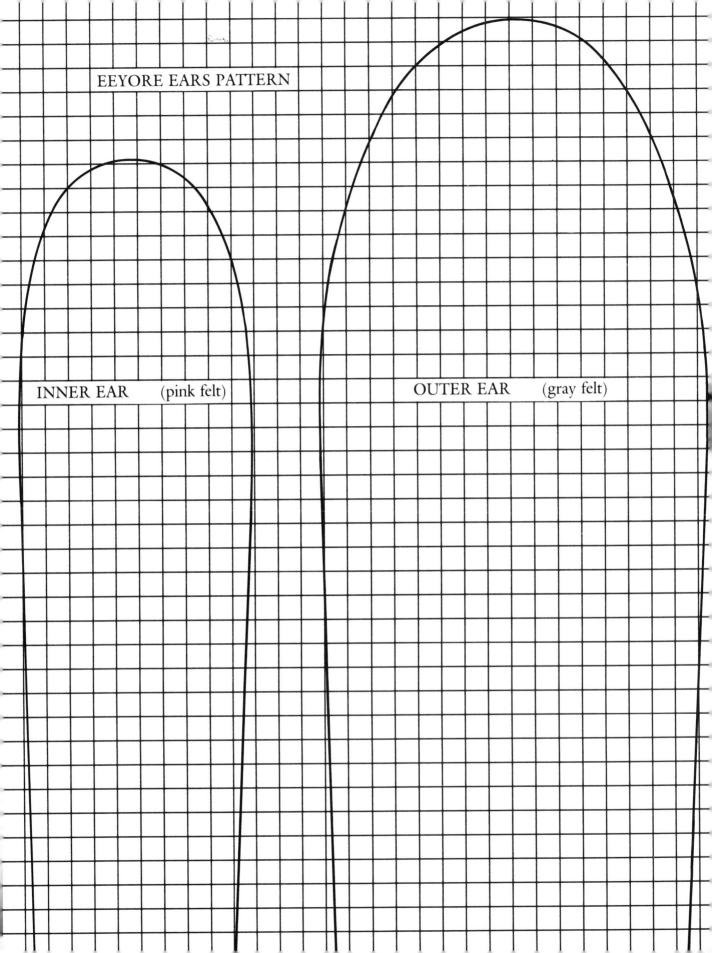

EEYORE EARS PATTERN

INNER EAR   (pink felt)

OUTER EAR   (gray felt)

Donkey Tails

Materials

36 yds. heavy-gauge gray yarn
2 yds. pink ribbon
12 large safety pins (old-fashioned diaper pins are a good choice)

Directions

Cut the yarn into 36 1-yard lengths. Cut the ribbon into 12 6″ lengths. For each tail, take three pieces of yarn, knot them in the middle, and put the pin through the knot (fig. 1). Braid the yarn into a tail, using two strands at a time (fig. 2). Tie a knot in the tail, about 4″ from the end. Tie the ribbon in a bow above the bottom knot (fig. 3). Help children pin the tails on the back of their clothing.

Preparation time for ears: 1 hour
Preparation time for tails: 45 minutes

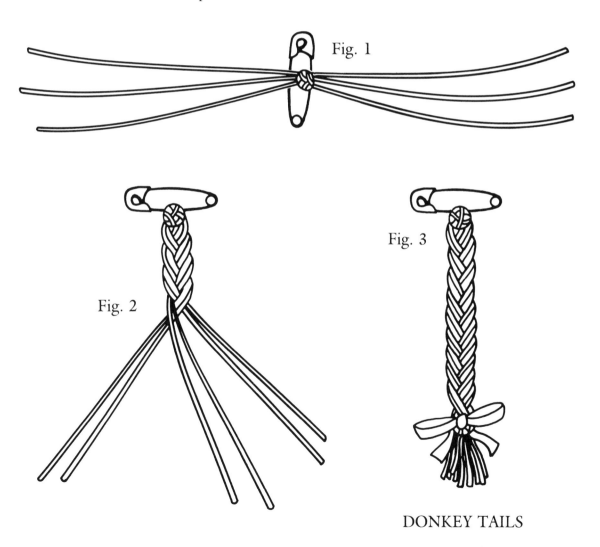

Fig. 1

Fig. 2

Fig. 3

DONKEY TAILS

G A M E S

Tigger Tag

With his springy tail, Tigger bounces through life. In Tigger Tag, everyone gets to bounce like Tigger. One child is designated Tigger or "it." All of the children hop around, and Tigger hops after them. When Tigger touches a player, that person must sit down right where he or she was tagged. When the last player left bouncing is tagged, the round is over, and this player becomes Tigger for the next round. The game continues until everyone is all bounced out.

Hide the Honey from the Heffalumps

In this game, Pooh tries to hide his honey from the heffalumps, which look suspiciously like elephants. Pooh's honey is kept—where else?—in one of those bear-shaped clear plastic bottles filled with honey. (For the purposes of this game, an empty bottle will work best—no sticky accidents!) One child is Pooh, and all the others are heffalumps. The heffalumps turn their backs and hide their heads in their trunks—that is, under their arms. Meanwhile, Pooh searches the yard or house for a good hiding place. When he's ready, he yells, "Oh, bother. I'm all out of honey." The heffalumps search for the honey. The one who finds it becomes Pooh, and Pooh becomes a heffalump. The cycle continues until most of the players have had a chance to hide the honey.

Roo Toss

As Kanga hopped around the Hundred-Acre Wood, she carried Roo around in her pouch. For this activity, children toss their Baby Roo Jelly-bean Bags into Kanga's pouch.

Find a large appliance box and draw or paint a kangaroo on it. Cut a hole out of the box where Kanga's pouch would be. Put a pillow inside the box to cushion the landing of the bean bags that land in the pouch. Children should take turns trying to toss their bags into Kanga's pouch. At the end of three rounds, the child with the most successful tosses is the winner. In case of a tie, you can hold a toss-off. For mishaps, such as spilled jelly beans, have extra jelly beans on hand for children to refill their bags.

Menu

O R A N G E - P I N E A P P L E O W L S

12 servings

Mandarin oranges, pineapple rings, raisins, and marshmallows make very wise owl salads!

Ingredients

12 lettuce leaves (green leaf)
12 canned-pineapple rings, drained
1 15-oz. can mandarin orange segments, drained
2 doz. large marshmallows
2 doz. raisins

ORANGE-PINEAPPLE OWLS

Directions

Arrange the pineapple rings on the lettuce leaves. Place two orange segments at the top of each pineapple ring to resemble the feather tufts of a great horned owl. Flatten marsh-mallows into ¼″ patties. Place on the pineapple rings for eyes. Use raisins for pupils, pushing them into the marshmallows. Place an orange segment (so that it tucks into the open space below the eyes) on the pineapple for a beak.

Note: These should be assembled at serving time on paper salad plates.

Preparation time: 15 minutes

POOH BEAR'S BURGER BISCUITS

(with Honey Mustard)

12 servings

Ingredients

4 cans extralarge refrigerated biscuits (8 count)
1 egg, beaten with 1 tbs. water
4 doz. blanched almonds
6 doz. raisins
2 doz. 1-oz. hamburger patties
Honey Mustard (use store-bought or see recipe that follows)

Directions

Open the cans and separate the biscuits. Place twenty-four biscuits on ungreased baking sheets, about 2″ apart. Cut each remaining biscuit into three equal-size pieces (fig. 1). Brush whole biscuits with egg, and roll biscuit pieces into balls. Press one ball into the center of each biscuit, and lightly brush with egg. Push two almonds, pointed ends out, into the top of each biscuit for ears. Use raisins for the eyes and nose (fig. 2). Bake in a preheated 400°F oven for about twelve minutes, and then split each biscuit in half. Grill or broil hamburger patties, and serve on biscuits with pots of Honey Mustard on the table.

Note: Biscuits are best served fresh and should be prepared on the day of the party.

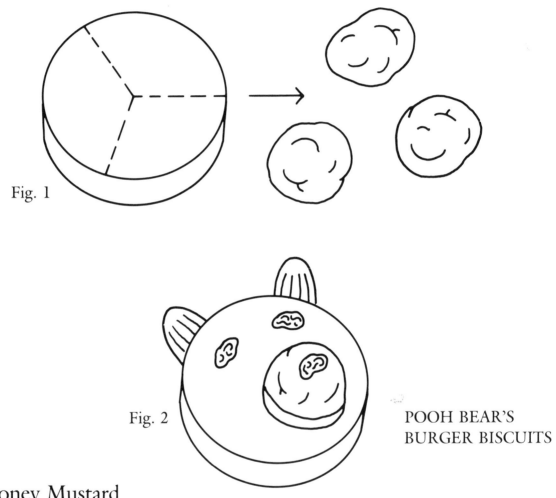

Fig. 1

Fig. 2

POOH BEAR'S
BURGER BISCUITS

Honey Mustard

Ingredients

1 cup golden brown mustard
½ cup honey
½ cup regular or nonfat mayonnaise
1 tbs. lemon juice

Directions
Blend the ingredients together until smooth, and store in the refrigerator until serving time.

Preparation time: 25 minutes
Baking time: 12 minutes

PIGLET'S PINK POTATO SALAD

12 servings

Piglet's potato salad gets its rosy hue from a dash of catsup. Piglet figures, why not? He always puts catsup on his french-fried potatoes.

Ingredients
9 medium boiling potatoes, washed and peeled
salted water
2 cups regular or nonfat mayonnaise
½ cup catsup
1 tsp. Worcestershire sauce
¼ cup chopped bread-and-butter pickles
½ cup chopped scallions
½ cup chopped celery
½ tsp. celery salt

Directions
Cut the potatoes into 1″ cubes, and boil them in salted water for about twenty minutes. Drain and chill. Meanwhile, combine the remaining ingredients, and blend with a wire whisk. Toss the dressing with the chilled potatoes, and chill finished potato salad overnight to allow flavors to develop.

Preparation time: 20 minutes
Chilling time: 8 to 24 hours

PEANUT BUTTER POOH CAKE

12 servings

Ingredients
1⅓ cups flour
1¼ tsp. baking powder
¼ tsp. salt
2 tbs. butter or margarine, softened
¼ cup peanut butter
1 cup firmly packed brown sugar
¼ cup sugar
1 tsp. vanilla
1 egg
⅔ cup milk
Peanut Butter Frosting (recipe follows)
2 small black gumdrops
1 large black gumdrop
black licorice laces (optional)

Directions
Grease and flour a 6-oz. glass ovenproof custard cup. Line an 8″-round cake pan with baking parchment. Stir the flour, baking powder, and salt together in a small mixing bowl. In a large mixing bowl, cream butter, peanut butter, and sugars together with an electric mixer. Beat in vanilla and egg. On a low speed, beat in the flour mixture and milk, alternately adding a little bit of each and ending with the flour. Beat until just combined. Fill the custard cup halfway with batter, and pour the remaining batter into the cake pan. Bake both cakes in a preheated 350°F oven for twenty to twenty-five minutes or until a toothpick inserted in the center of the cakes comes out clean. Cool the cakes for ten minutes, and then invert them on a wire rack. Peel the parchment from the back of the 8″ layer, and allow the cakes to cool completely. Cut the custard-cup cake horizontally into thirds (fig. 1). Cut a ½″ piece from each of those bottom circles to make Pooh's ears (fig. 2). Use the top section of the cake for Pooh Bear's snout. On a large round platter arrange the cakes as shown in figure 3. Cover with Peanut Butter Frosting. Use two small gumdrops for Pooh's eyes, one large gumdrop for his nose, and if you want, licorice laces for his mouth and eyebrows (fig. 4).

Peanut Butter Frosting

Ingredients
4½ cups confectioners' sugar
½ cup peanut butter
⅓ to ½ cup milk

12

Directions

Cream the confectioners' sugar with the peanut butter and enough milk to make a frosting of smooth spreading consistency.

Note: This cake freezes very well and may be prepared up to three weeks in advance. Place uncovered cake in freezer, and after one hour, when frosting has gotten firm, cover whole cake in plastic.

Preparation time: 45 minutes
Baking time: 20 to 25 minutes

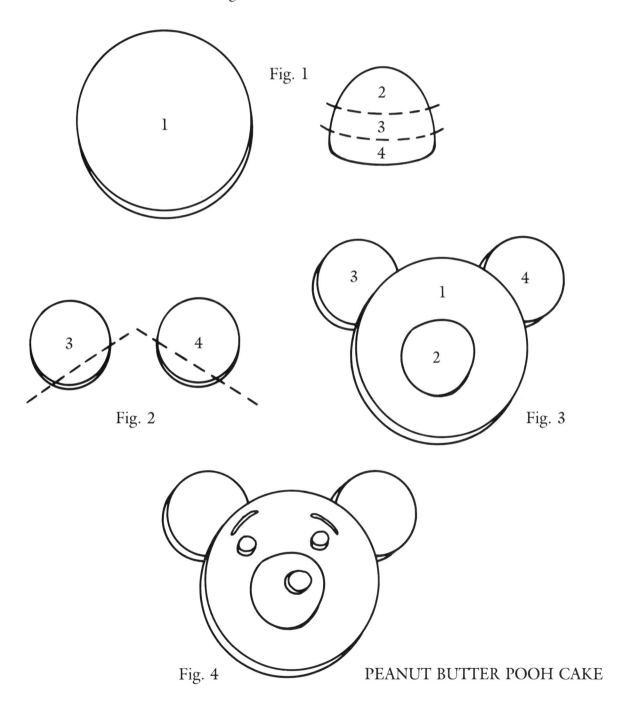

Fig. 1

Fig. 2

Fig. 3

Fig. 4   PEANUT BUTTER POOH CAKE

F R O Z E N   T I G G E R S

12 servings

Ingredients
1½ gals. orange sherbert
2 doz. miniature marshmallows
2 doz. small orange gumdrops
1½ cups fudge sauce (any brand that becomes thickened and firm when frozen)

Directions
Cover a large cookie sheet with aluminum foil. Work quickly, evenly spacing twelve large round scoops of sherbert on the foil. Make smaller scoops with a miniature ice-cream scoop or melon baller, and push each one into the base of a large scoop. The small scoop will serve as Tigger's snout. Above the small scoop, press two marshmallows into the large scoop for eyes. Flatten gumdrops with your fingers, and press two into each large scoop for ears (fig. 1). Fill a pastry bag, fitted with a #3 small round writing tip, with fudge sauce. Pipe a nose and mouth on each Tigger. Pipe pupils on the marshmallow eyes and stripes on the top and sides of his head (fig. 2). Return the sherbert to the freezer at least three hours before serving time.

Note: Frozen Tiggers may be prepared up to three days in advance if stored in a covered container or wrapped in plastic once firmly frozen.

Preparation time: 15 minutes
Freezing time: 3 hours to 3 days

Fig. 1

Fig. 2

FROZEN TIGGERS

HUNDRED-ACRE WOOD HONEY APPLE PUNCH

12 servings

Ingredients
1 gal. apple cider or apple juice
1 6-oz. can frozen lemonade concentrate
½ cup honey
1 2-liter bottle club soda or sparkling water, chilled

Directions
Fill three ice cube trays with apple cider. Freeze for at least five hours, until firm. Combine remaining cider with lemonade and honey. Pour in club soda. This is fun to ladle from a large pot or crock into cups filled with apple-cider ice.

Preparation time: 10 minutes
Freezing time: 5 hours

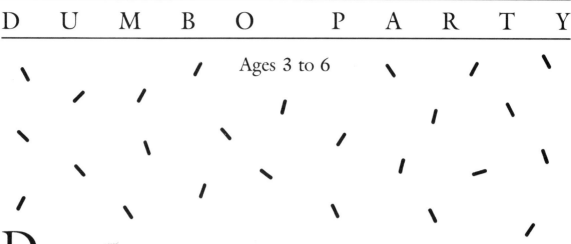

Ages 3 to 6

Disney's fourth animated film, *Dumbo*, is the story of a baby circus elephant with enormous ears. Because of his ears, Dumbo is ridiculed by all the other circus animals, except for his good friend, the streetwise Timothy Mouse. But when he discovers that his ears make dandy wings, the teasing turns to cheering for the world's first flying elephant.

Invitation: Circus Baby Bundles

Decorations: Circus Motif—striped-sheet circus tent; balloons; stuffed circus animals; paper-tube trapeze; yellow cellophane straw; unshelled peanuts

Get-acquainted Activity: Clown Balloons

Fantasy Feature: Elephant Ears

Games: Pyramid of Pachyderms; Flight of the Magic Feather; Ringmaster

Menu: Orange Elephants; Cheesy Clownwiches; Dumbo Dip; Sorbet Balloon Bouquets; Dumbo and the Pink Elephant Cakes; Timothy's Tutti-frutti Punch

Circus Baby Bundles

In the film *Dumbo* a very important event takes place every spring at the circus. A flock of storks drops baby bundles down from the sky over the circus tents. Each package contains an animal baby and is addressed to a circus mother. It was just such a special delivery that brought Dumbo and his mother, Mrs. Jumbo, together.

The circus babies used in these invitation bundles are animal crackers, making these the type of invitations best delivered by hand. They can, however, also be mailed in a small box or padded envelope.

Materials
12 paper napkins (blue and/or pink)
96–120 animal crackers
curling ribbon
12 3″ × 5″ unruled cards
paper hole punch
blue and/or pink felt-tip markers

Directions
Fold each card in half. On the outside write "TO: (name of child invited)." On the inside write the following:

This bundle of circus babies
is your invitation to the Big Top
Please come to (your address)
on (date) at (time)
for (your child's name)'s birthday
RSVP: (your phone number)

CIRCUS
BABY
BUNDLES

Punch a hole at the corner of the folded edge of each card, and thread the ribbon through the card. Place eight to ten assorted animal crackers in the center of each napkin square. Bring the ends together, and tie them with the ribbon. Curl the ribbon, if desired.

Preparation time: 40 minutes

Naturally, you'll want to hold this event under a big top. It's simple to suggest a circus tent with striped sheets or paper tablecloths. Indoors, you can drape the tent from the ceiling. Outdoors, string a clothesline from two posts (or trees), and drape your material pup-tent style. Use stakes and string to anchor the sides into the ground. If you have a long picnic table, you can attach poles at each end and make a modest canopy to cover the table. A circus also calls for an abundance of balloons, which should be hung everywhere. Place stuffed circus animals around the room or yard. You can even rig a decorative trapeze from the ceiling or a tree. Use wrapping-paper tubes (covered with paper) for a trapeze swing. Suspend the swing from ribbons over a fishnet.

   Cover the party table with yellow cellophane straw and unshelled roasted peanuts. (Opening peanuts helps keep hungry kids busy.) For the three-ring-circus effect, place the Dumbo Cake in the center and one Pink Elephant Cake at each end of the table. To make place settings, use paper cups filled with popcorn. Write one child's name on each cup.

G E T - A C Q U A I N T E D   A C T I V I T Y

Clown Balloons

For the opening activity, children decorate balloons to make them look like clown heads. Set up an area for the makeup tent with a bouquet of white balloons and several sets of colored felt-tip markers. (Use flat-tip markers; they're less likely to pop balloons.) As children arrive, let them create faces to suit their fancy. You might want to make up a sample balloon for very young children, showing curly orange hair, a bright red nose, and a big smiling mouth.

Preparation time: 15 minutes

CLOWN BALLOON

Elephant Ears

Dumbo's oversize ears are his most distinctive feature. You can make them out of either blue or gray paper and poster board.

Materials
1 20″ × 30″ sheet gray or blue poster board
20″ × 2½ yds. gray or blue crepe paper
ruler
pencil
scissors
stapler
glitter paint in writing tube

Directions
Cut the poster board into twelve 2″ × 20″ strips. Staple the strips together to form headbands, overlapping the ends (fig. 1). Use your child as a guide for average head size. Cut twenty-four 12″ diameter circles from the crepe paper, and make a pinch pleat at the top of each circle to resemble ears (fig. 2). Staple ears to the outside of each band (fig. 3). Use the glitter to write each child's name across the front of the headband (fig. 4).

Preparation time: 1 hour

ELEPHANT EARS

Fig. 1

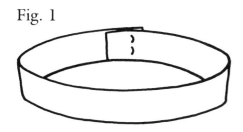

Fig. 2

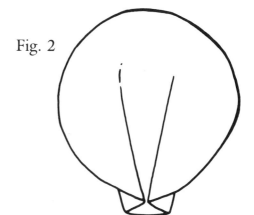

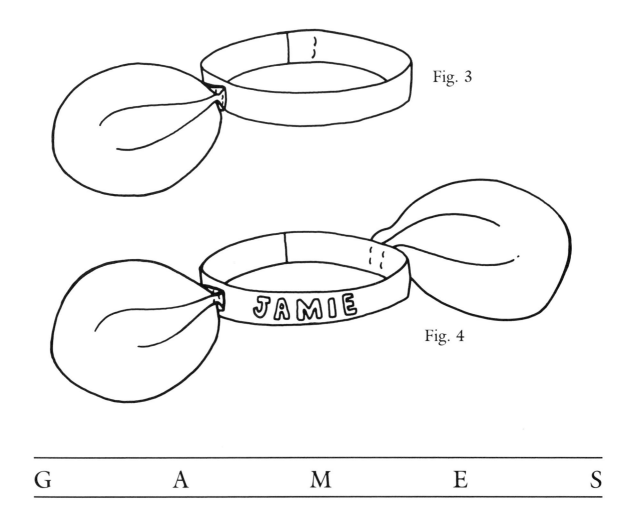

Fig. 3

Fig. 4

JAMIE

G A M E S

Pyramid of Pachyderms

Poor Dumbo was demoted to circus clown after he toppled a tower of elephants. As he tried to spring to the top of the pyramid, he tripped on his giant ears, and the elephants came tumbling down!

Any child who's ever seen a cheerleading team knows how to get on hands and knees and build a pyramid. This formation is usually performed by a group of six (three on the bottom, two on the second row, and one on top). However, small children may find this a bit too challenging. A simple pyramid of three is just as much fun.

Begin by dividing the children into four groups of three. (If you don't have a soft carpet or grassy surface, provide mats to cushion their knees.) At a given signal, each group forms a pyramid. Two children get down on hands and knees, side by side. The third (and preferably smallest) child climbs on top and centers him- or herself between the other two. To add drama to this balancing act, place a small stuffed animal on the back of the top child. The object of the game is to see which pyramid can hold up the longest.

DUMBO PARTY—Dumbo and the Pink Elephant Cakes (p. 27)

Flight of the Magic Feather

Timothy Mouse gave Dumbo the confidence to fly by telling him that his secret power came from a magic feather. As long as Dumbo held the feather in his trunk, he soared through the air with ease. But when he dropped it during a flight, Dumbo nearly crashed to the ground. However, he continued his flight without the feather and realized that he never needed the feather to fly at all.

For this game, you will need two feathers, available at craft or hobby stores. Begin by splitting the children up into two teams. Choose a goal line or end marker that is some distance from the starting line. Each team forms a line, and the two teams stand side by side. The first player on each team places a feather behind his or her ear and, at the signal, runs to the goal line and back. He or she then passes the feather on to the next person in line. Players can "fly" only as long as their feathers stay positioned behind their ears. If a feather drops or blows away, the child must stop, pick up the feather, and finish the course by crawling on hands and knees. The first team to finish becomes "The World's Fastest Flying Elephants!"

Ringmaster

All you need for the Ringmaster game is a hoop. To begin, one child is picked to be the ringmaster, and he or she must hold the hoop. The rest of the children are dancing bears. The ringmaster begins by holding the hoop up so that the bottom of it touches the ground. The bears take turns jumping through the hoop, which is progressively raised, inch by inch, after each round. If a bear doesn't make it through the hoop, he or she becomes the next ringmaster, and the hoop is lowered again.

Menu

ORANGE ELEPHANTS

12 servings

Ingredients
12 navel oranges
4 doz. large marshmallows
toothpicks (see note, page x)
2 doz. miniature marshmallows
2 doz. whole cloves

Directions

For each elephant, make a V cut just above the orange's stem end for the tail (fig. 1). Carve a Y at the other end for the trunk (fig. 2). At each side, make C-shaped cuts for ears. Gently pull all cut peel slightly away from the orange (fig. 3). With toothpicks, attach four large marshmallows to the bottom of each orange for legs. Flatten the miniature marshmallows to form the eyes. Insert clove stems for pupils through the center of each marshmallow, and push them into place on the orange (fig. 4).

Note: These are best prepared the morning of the party.

Preparation time: 25 minutes

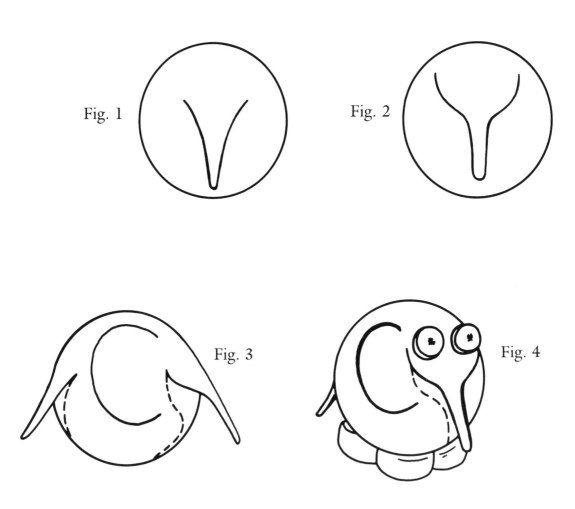

Fig. 1

Fig. 2

Fig. 3

Fig. 4

ORANGE ELEPHANTS

CHEESY CLOWNWICHES

24 sandwiches

Ingredients
24 slices firm-textured white bread
3 8-oz. tubs soft-spread cream cheese
2 cans cheese spread
12 cherry tomatoes
12 red bell pepper rings or slices
12 to 14 pimento-stuffed olives, sliced

Directions
Use a 4"- or 5"-round cookie cutter to trim the bread slices into circles. Spread an even layer of cream cheese over each slice. Squeeze cheese spread along one rim of each slice to resemble curly clown hair (fig. 1). Split the cherry tomatoes in half, draining the seeds. Place a tomato half, cut side down, in the center of each sandwich for a clown nose. Cut each bell pepper ring into two semicircles, and use each piece for a smiling clown mouth. Use slices of the stuffed olives for eyes (fig. 2).

Note: These open-faced sandwiches are best prepared right before serving so the bread doesn't dry out.

Preparation time: 30 minutes

CHEESY CLOWNWICHES

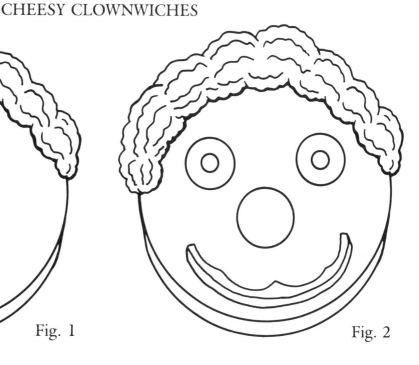

Fig. 1   Fig. 2

D U M B O   D I P

A large squash shaped like an elephant's head serves as the holder for this tasty dip.

Ingredients
1 large yellow crooked-neck squash (neck should be curved, base should be bulbous)
toothpicks (see note, page x)
2 whole cloves
ornamental kale (or ruffled salad-bowl lettuce leaf)
potato chips, carrots, celery, and cucumber strips, for dipping
Dumbo Dip (recipe follows)

Directions
Cut the stem from the end of the squash neck, and then cut horizontal slices for both the top and bottom of the base (fig. 1). Be careful *not* to cut through the bottom of the squash. Anchor the slices to the sides of the squash with toothpicks to form ears. Cut indentations for the eyes and nostrils. Insert cloves into the eyes (fig. 2). Using the cut mark at the top of the head for a guide, hollow out a cavity in the squash, and fill it with the dip. Place the elephant in the middle of a serving platter on top of a curly leaf of kale or lettuce, arranged to resemble a clown ruff (fig. 3). Set out potato chips and vegetables around the elephant. Additional dip can be spooned into cups and served on luncheon plates (the head doesn't really hold that much).

Note: The squash shell may be prepared the night before if you brush the exposed cut surfaces with lemon juice. Cover it with plastic wrap, and store it in the refrigerator. Fill with dip just before serving.

Dumbo Dip

Ingredients
1 pt. cottage cheese
½ cup regular or nonfat sour cream
½ cup regular or nonfat mayonnaise
¼ cup chopped parsley
1 tbs. fresh-snipped chives (or 1 tsp. dried)
1 tbs. fresh-snipped parsley (or 1 tsp. dried)
½ cup chopped cucumber, peeled and seeded
1 tsp. herb-seasoned salt

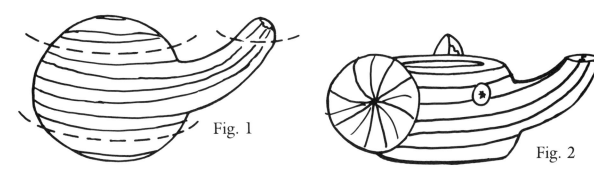

Fig. 1

Fig. 2

Fig. 3

Directions

Combine all the ingredients in a mixing bowl until blended. Chill at least eight hours to allow flavors to develop.

Note: Dip may be prepared up to three days in advance.

Preparation time: 25 minutes
Chilling time: 8 hours or longer

SORBET BALLOON BOUQUETS

12 servings

Sorbet Balloon Bouquets is a light dessert that can also be made with frozen yogurt in flavors of bright contrasting colors. Licorice laces give the effect of a balloon bouquet. The bouquet is served just as you prepare it. So simple, there's no need to make it in advance.

Ingredients
3 doz. 10″ black licorice laces
1 pt. lime sorbet (or sherbert)
1 pt. raspberry sorbet (or sherbert)
1 pt. orange sorbet (or sherbert)

Directions
For each bouquet, hold three licorice laces together, and knot them at one end. Arrange them on a serving plate, fanning out the laces. Using a miniature ice-cream scoop or melon baller, place a different flavor of sorbet at the end of each licorice lace. Serve at once.

Preparation time: 10 minutes

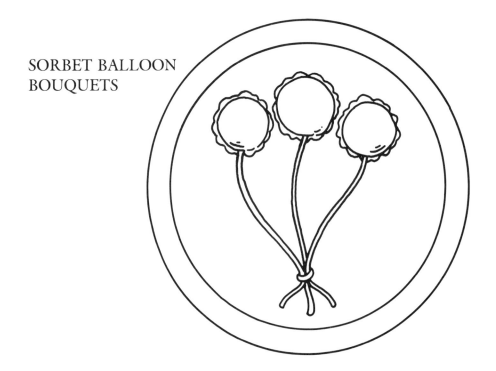

SORBET BALLOON
BOUQUETS

DUMBO AND THE PINK ELEPHANT CAKES

For a Dumbo party, I like to set the cakes up as a three-ring circus: a pink-frosted elephant cake at each end of the table, and a blue-frosted Dumbo cake with a feather in its trunk in the center. This recipe yields enough for three elephant cakes.

Ingredients

2¼ cups flour
1⅔ cups sugar
⅔ cup shortening
¾ cup milk
½ cup Maraschino cherry juice from cherry jar
3½ tsp. baking powder
1 tsp. salt
5 egg whites
2 doz. chopped Maraschino cherries
Creamy Cherry Frosting (recipe follows)
Basic Frosting (for blue and black icing, recipe follows)
6 large marshmallows
flat-bottomed ice-cream cone
colored feather (from craft store)

Directions

Beat the flour, sugar, shortening, milk, cherry juice, baking powder, and salt in a large bowl until blended. Turn the electric mixer on high speed, and beat the mixture for two minutes. Add the egg whites and beat for two minutes longer. Fold in the cherries. Line three 8″-round cake pans with baking parchment and divide the batter evenly among the pans. Bake in a preheated 350°F oven for twenty-five to thirty minutes or until a toothpick inserted in the center of the cakes comes out clean. Cool completely, then gently invert the pans and peel the parchment from the cakes.

Cover three 14″-round boards with foil (or use very large plates). Cut each cake according to figure 1, and arrange the pieces on the plates to resemble elephant heads (fig. 2). Cover two cakes with pink frosting and the remaining cake with blue frosting. Place two marshmallow eyes on each cake. Fill a small pastry bag, fitted with a #3 round writing tip, with black frosting. Pipe pupils on the eyes (fig. 3) and nostrils at the end of the trunks (fig. 4). For Dumbo (the blue cake), stick the feather in the end of his trunk. Invert the ice-cream cone on Dumbo's head for a hat. Put spare blue (or pink) frosting in a pastry bag and write "DUMBO" on the hat (fig. 5).

Note: These cakes may be prepared two weeks in advance and frozen. Wrap them in plastic after the frosting has firmed in the freezer for an hour.

Creamy Cherry Frosting

Ingredients
4 cups confectioners' sugar
½ cup butter or margarine
½ cup shortening
3 tbs. Maraschino cherry juice
1 tbs. milk
1 tsp. almond extract
red gel food coloring

Directions
Beat the ingredients together until the frosting is a smooth, spreadable consistency. Add additional milk if necessary. Tint the mixture pink with red food coloring.

Basic Frosting

Ingredients
¼ cup butter or margarine, softened
¼ cup shortening
2 cups confectioners' sugar
2 tbs. milk
½ tsp. almond extract
blue and black gel food colorings

Directions
Beat the ingredients together until the frosting is a smooth, spreadable consistency. Add additional milk if necessary. Reserve ¼ cup of frosting, leaving it white for the moment. If you need more blue or black frosting, you can tint accordingly. Tint 3 tbs. of the frosting black. Tint the remaining frosting blue.

 Preparation time: 45 minutes
Baking time: 25 to 30 minutes

DUMBO AND THE PINK
ELEPHANT CAKES

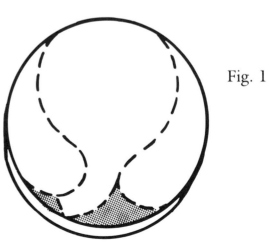

Fig. 1

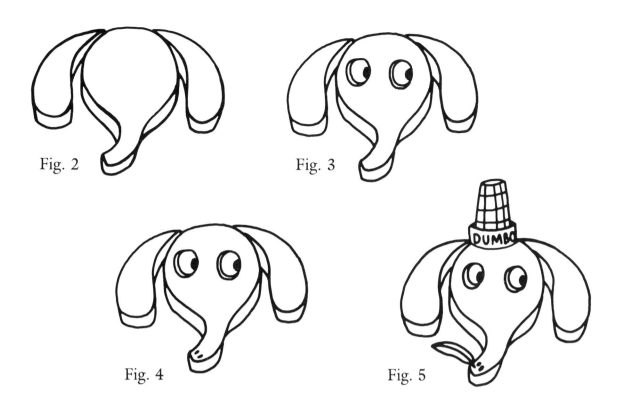

Fig. 2

Fig. 3

Fig. 4

Fig. 5

T I M O T H Y ' S   T U T T I - F R U T T I P U N C H

12 servings

Brightly colored fruit-flavored ice cubes carry out the balloon bouquet theme.

Ingredients
1 pt. orange juice
1 pt. Concord grape juice
1 pt. limeade
1 3-liter bottle ginger ale or other noncola soft drink, chilled

Directions
Pour each flavor of juice into separate ice cube trays, and freeze them for at least six hours until firm. Just before serving, divide the ice cubes among the cups with at least one cube of each color per cup. Pour soft drink over the top.

Preparation time: 10 minutes
Freezing time: 6 hours or longer

101 DALMATIANS PUPPY PARTY

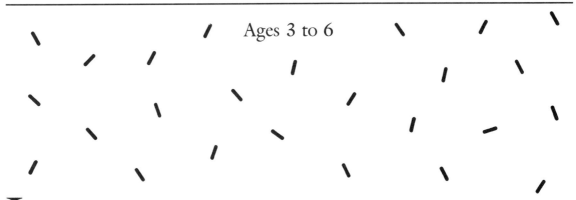

Ages 3 to 6

In the 1961 Walt Disney film *101 Dalmatians,* the Dalmatians Pongo and Perdita must outwit the diabolical Cruella de Vil. Cruella has kidnapped every Dalmatian puppy in London, including Pongo and Perdita's fifteen pups, in order to make herself a fur coat! With the help of a canine network called the Twilight Bark, the brave couple manages to free ninety-nine puppies from the clutches of Cruella and her bumbling henchmen.

Invitation: Dalmatian

Decorations: Polka-dot Puppy Motif—spotted tablecloth; polka-dot balloons, plates, and cups; personalized pet bowls

Get-acquainted Activity: Dog Biscuit Bakeshop

Fantasy Feature: Dalmatian Dog Ears and Personalized Dog Collars

Games: The Twilight Bark; Buried Bones; Dog Catcher

Menu: Pongo's Pears; Hot Dogs in Bread-bone Buns; Canine Crunchies; Perdita's Chipper Ice-cream Pups; Dalmatian Cake; Polka-dot Milk

Dalmatian

A smiling polka-dot puppy invites guests to this party at the Dalmatian Plantation, a place just swarming with puppies!

Materials
12 9″ × 12″ sheets white poster board
4-yd. roll ¾″ red plastic tape
12 1½″ to 2″ gold notary seals
black felt-tip marker
12 9″ × 12″ white envelopes

Directions
For each invitation cut a 12″ strip of tape and press it down onto the long side of the poster board, about 2″ from the bottom (fig. 1). Fold the poster board in half and stick a notary seal in the middle of the tape on the front. This becomes a collar. Draw a dog face on each card and write the name of the child to whom the invitation is addressed on the tag (fig. 2). Draw spots all over the front and back of the card and on the back of the envelope (fig. 3). Write the following message inside each card:

Pongo, Perdita, and (your child's name)
are having a Polka-dot Puppy Party
at
The Dalmatian Plantation
(your address)
on (date) at (time)
Rooof!SVP: (your phone number)

Preparation time: 1 hour 20 minutes

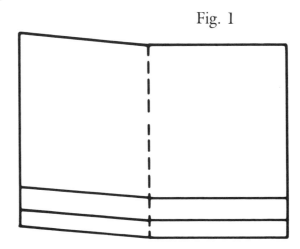

Fig. 1

Fig. 2

Fig. 3

D E C O R A T I O N S

For Dalmatian decorations, think dots! Use acrylic black paint to sponge spots all over a white paper tablecloth. Then paint nontoxic polka dots on sturdy white paper (or plastic) plates and cups. You can even cover white balloons with black spots. As a centerpiece, the Dalmatian Cake takes the spotlight. You can serve Canine Crunchies in unique place settings: small plastic pet bowls, each personalized with a different child's name.

G E T - A C Q U A I N T E D   A C T I V I T Y

Dog Biscuit Bakeshop

Kids love playing with modeling clay—especially when it's edible! For this activity, children mold sugar cookie dough (studded with chocolate chips) into dog-bone-shaped cookies. Have miniature chips on hand so that cookies can be personalized with each child's name.

Ingredients

⅔ cup shortening
⅔ cup butter or margarine, softened
⅔ cup sugar
½ tsp. almond extract
3⅓ cups flour
1 6-oz. bag semisweet chocolate chips
1 6-oz. bag miniature semisweet chocolate chips

Directions

Cream the shortening, butter, sugar, and almond extract together until smooth. Blend in the flour. Mix regular-size chocolate chips into the dough. (Miniature chips are for decorating.) Divide the dough into twelve equal-size balls. Cover them in plastic wrap and chill. Dough should be softened at room temperature one hour before the party.

When guests arrive, bring each child to the table set up for the Dog Biscuit Bakeshop. Place a ball of dough in the center of a paper plate, and let each child mold it into a dog-bone shape. Set out a dish of miniature chips for children to spell out their names on their cookies. (Very small children will need help from an adult.) While children are eating lunch, transfer the bones to a cookie sheet lined with baking parchment. Bake them in a preheated 300°F oven for twenty-five to thirty minutes. The edges should be firm but the cookies not browned. Let them cool completely, then carefully remove them from the paper. Wrap the cookies in plastic wrap for children to take home.

Note: This dough may be prepared up to a week in advance.

Preparation time: 15 minutes
Chilling time: only necessary for storing
Baking time: 25 to 30 minutes

DOG BISCUIT BAKESHOP

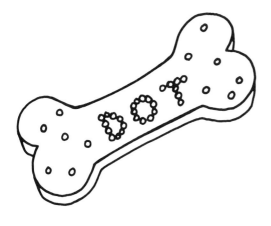
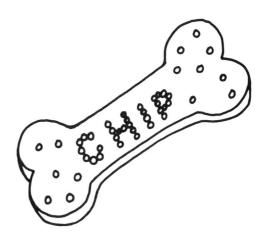

Dalmatian Dog Ears and Personalized Dog Collars

Small children love to pretend that they're animals. Donning Dalmatian Dog Ears and dog collars helps put kids in the mood for make-believe.

Materials
2 yds. white felt
tracing paper
1 sheet thin poster board
pencil
rubber cement
black fabric paint
sponge
scissors
stapler

Directions
Cut twelve 2″-wide and 24″-long strips of felt for headbands. Using your child as a guide, wrap the felt band around his or her head, and staple the two ends together in the back (fig. 1). There should be an overlap of 3″ to 4″. With tracing paper and pencil trace the dog ears pattern on page 35. Cut out the tracing, glue it to the poster board, and cut out the stencil. Use the stencil to cut out 24 Dalmatian Dog Ears. Fold a pleat in each ear (fig. 2), and staple two to the inside of each headband. The ears should drop over the top of the band. Dip the tip of the sponge into the black paint, and dot the ears and headband all over to make Dalmatian spots (fig. 3). Allow the dog ears to dry for approximately twenty-four hours.

Preparation time: 1 hour
Drying time: 24 hours

Fig. 1

Fig. 2

Fig. 3

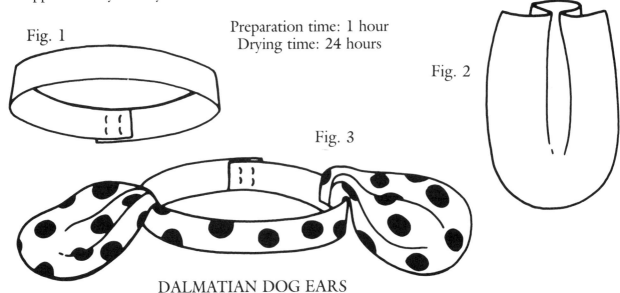

DALMATIAN DOG EARS

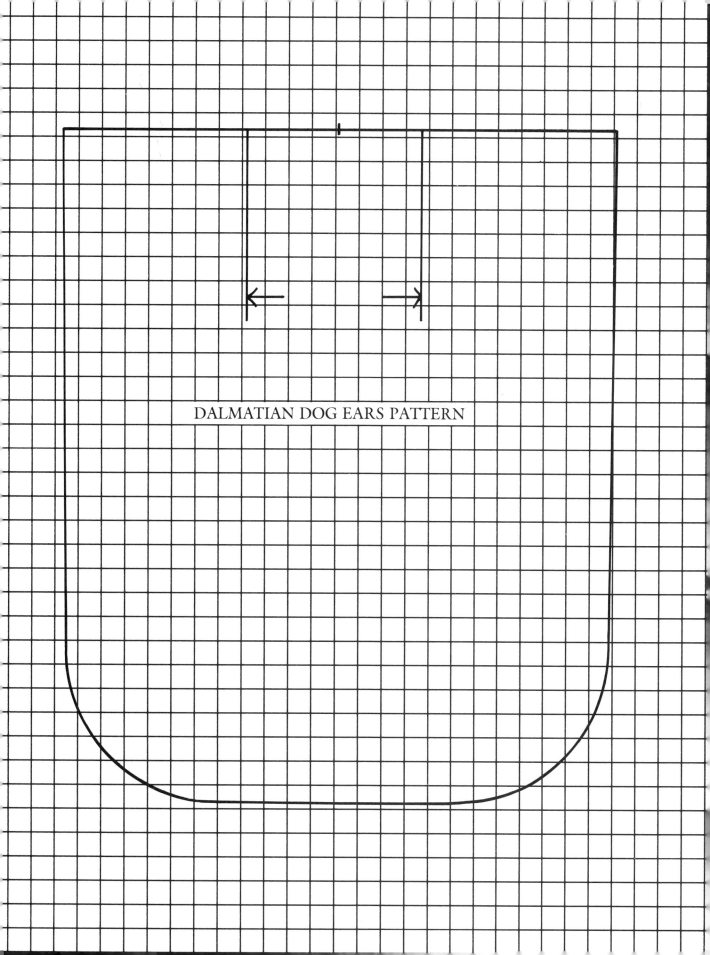

DALMATIAN DOG EARS PATTERN

Materials

5 yds. 1″ red gross-grain ribbon
12 jumbo paper clips (brass plated or red-enamel coated)
24 1½″-2″ self-adhesive gold notary seals
paper hole punch
scissors
black felt-tip laundry marker
stapler

Directions

Cut twelve 15″ strips of ribbon. Punch a hole in the center of each strip. Hook a paper clip through the hole (fig. 1), then stick two gold seals back to back so that you have twelve gold dog tags. Punch holes in the top of the tags and write one child's name on each tag (fig. 2). Hook the tags on to the paper clips (fig. 3). When the children arrive, staple collars around each child's neck, making sure the collars fit loosely and comfortably.

Preparation time: 45 minutes

PERSONALIZED DOG COLLARS

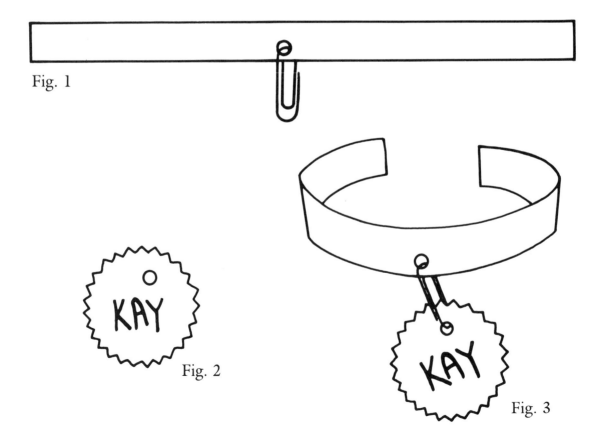

Fig. 1

Fig. 2

Fig. 3

101 DALMATIANS PARTY — Hot Dogs in Bread-bone Buns (p. 39) and Perdita's Chipper Ice-cream Pups (p. 41)

The Twilight Bark

From Danny the Great Dane to old Towser, to the Colonel and Sergeant Tibbs, the Twilight Bark was like a telegraph. Each dog barked word of the missing puppies clear down the river Thames (although sometimes the message got a little muddled, much the way it does in the game telephone).

Line the children up across the yard (or large room), about four feet apart from each other. The child at the beginning of the line thinks of a message, runs up to the next child, and whispers it in his or her ear. (For very young children, this is challenging enough. Slightly older players can use longer messages.) The message is passed down the line to the final child, who announces it aloud. Children will enjoy hearing how the message got changed along the way. The player at the end of the line moves to the front of the line and starts a new message. The Twilight Bark continues until each child gets a chance to send his or her own message.

Buried Bones

Essentially an Easter egg hunt, Buried Bones is played using dog biscuits instead of eggs. Buy a large box of multicolored dog biscuits (red, green, and brown). Hide them in secret places around the yard or house. Use an equal amount of each color. Divide the children into three teams: the red team, the green team, and the brown team. Each team goes in search of its bones. A bone in the team color is worth three points. A bone in another team's color is worth only one point. After all of the bones have been accounted for (or a reasonable period of time has elapsed), a tally is taken. The team scoring the most points wins.

Dog Catcher

Dog Catcher is a hide-and-seek game. The hiders are Dalmatians; the seeker is Cruella de Vil. Cruella carries a little goldfish net (symbolic of the classic dogcatcher's net). The Dalmatians run and hide in places throughout the yard or house while Cruella counts to 101. Younger children may want to count to ten, then add "101" at the end for good measure. When Cruella finds a Dalmatian, she brings it back to the mansion. The last Dalmatian to be caught is the winner. The first Dalmatian to be caught becomes Cruella in the next round.

Menu

P O N G O ' S   P E A R S

12 servings

Most small children love fruit salads. Canned pears and prunes make this one easy and economical.

Ingredients
12 lettuce leaves (green leaf or Boston)
12 premium-quality (large) canned pear halves
6 canned prunes
12 miniature marshmallows
12 raisins
6 Concord (purple) grapes

Directions
Place the lettuce leaves to one side of the lunch plates. (Hot Dogs in Bread-bone Buns will be served alongside this dish.) Drain the liquid from the pears, and place them cut side down on the lettuce leaves. Split the prunes in half, lengthwise, and remove the pits. Place the prune halves at large ends of pear halves for ears (fig. 1). Cut small holes in each pear for an eye and push in marshmallows. Press raisins in the marshmallows for the pupils. Split the grapes in half, crosswise, removing the seeds. Set one grape half at the end of each pear for a nose (fig. 2).

Note: These take so little time, there's no need to prepare them in advance.

Preparation time: 15 minutes

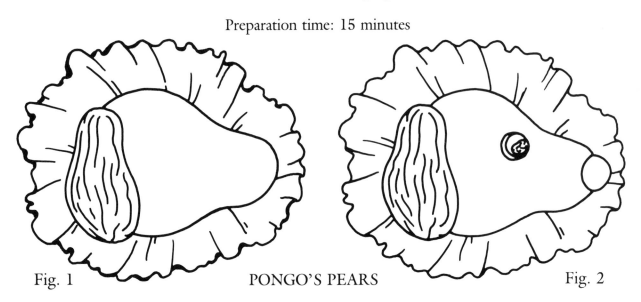

Fig. 1   PONGO'S PEARS   Fig. 2

HOT DOGS IN BREAD-BONE BUNS

These frankfurters, wrapped in bread sticks to resemble dog bones, will delight the Dalmatian pups at the party—even though they bake up big enough for a Saint Bernard!

Ingredients
12 frankfurters or turkey franks
3 cans (8 count) refrigerated bread sticks
1 egg
1 tbs. water

Directions
For each bone, unroll the bread sticks and wrap one around each frankfurter (fig. 1). Stretch the dough and pinch the seams together to completely conceal the frank (fig. 2). Unroll another bread stick for each frank and split it in half. Press the center of each strip firmly into the end of each frankfurter. Then roll the ends of the dough toward each other to resemble the knobs of a bone (fig. 3). Place bones 3″ apart on a baking sheet that has been sprayed with nonstick coating. Beat the egg with 1 tbs. water and brush each bone with the mixture. Bake in a preheated 350°F oven for twenty minutes or until they are puffy and brown (fig. 4). Serve them warm on plates with Pongo's Pears and condiments.

Note: These are best when wrapped and baked immediately before serving. The uncooked dough does not keep well in the refrigerator. If you must make these the night before, partially bake them for seventeen minutes. Refrigerate and then reheat them in a 250°F oven for ten or twelve minutes until golden brown and heated through.

Preparation time: 20 minutes
Baking time: 20 minutes

HOT DOGS IN BREAD-BONE BUNS

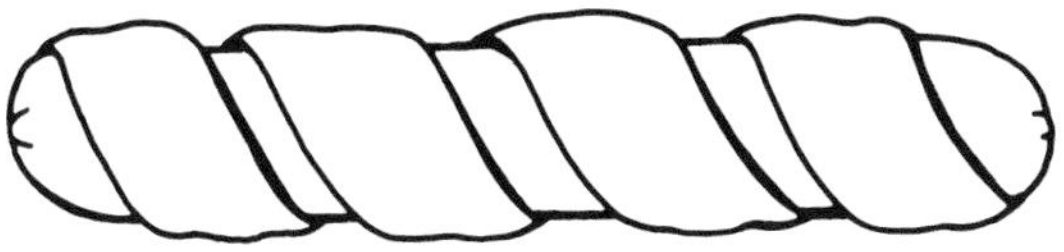

Fig. 1

Fig. 2

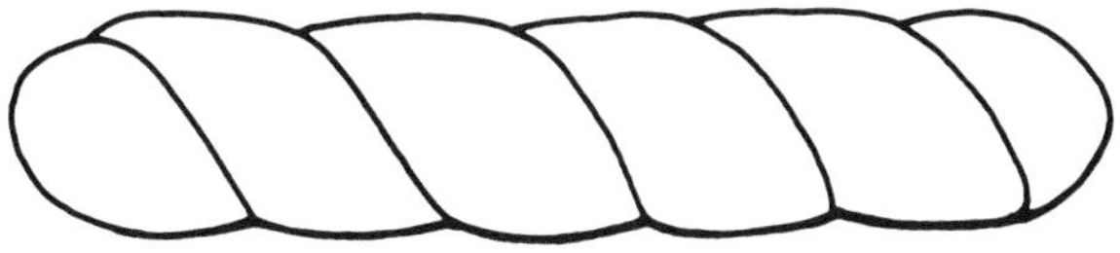

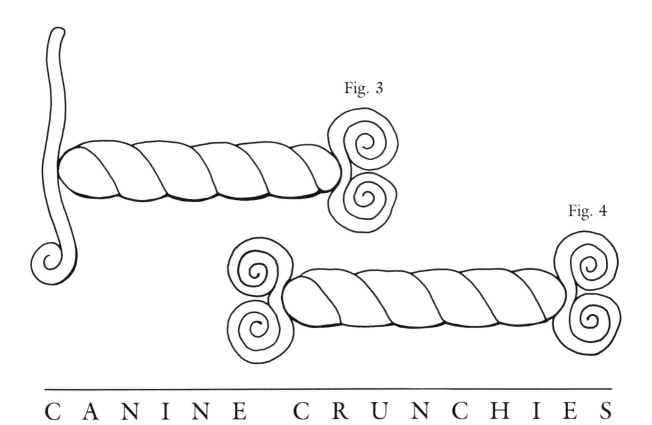

Fig. 3

Fig. 4

C A N I N E   C R U N C H I E S

Pongo and Perdita's pups love to watch television. Their favorite show is "Thunder," about a sheriff's dog of the Wild, Wild West, and their favorite commercial is for Canine Crunchies dog food.

At this party, Canine Crunchies can be anything your child likes: potato chips, corn chips, pretzels, popcorn, or a variety of these snacks mixed together. The secret ingredient is the box! Simply wrap an empty economy-size cereal box with construction paper. Then design your own logo for Canine Crunchies with crayons or felt-tip markers. Fill the box with the desired snacks and set it on the table (fig. 1). To serve, pour some into the personalized dog dishes described in the Decorations section (fig. 2).

Preparation time: 30 minutes

Fig. 1

Fig. 2

CANINE CRUNCHIES

40

PERDITA'S CHIPPER ICE-CREAM PUPS

12 servings

What's the ideal Dalmatian dessert? Why, chocolate-chip ice cream, of course!

Ingredients
½ gal. chocolate-chip ice cream
12 chocolate-covered mint patties, 1½″ in diameter
24 miniature marshmallows
1 cup dark-chocolate fudge sauce (any brand that becomes thickened and firm when frozen)

Directions
Cover a cookie sheet with aluminum foil. Working quickly, place twelve large scoops of ice cream about 3″ apart on the sheet. Push miniscoops of ice cream onto each large scoop for dog muzzles (fig. 1). Split the mint patties in half and push the cut sides into the scoops for ears. Push marshmallows into large scoops for eyes. Fill a small pastry bag, fitted with a #3 or #4 small round writing tip, with fudge sauce. Pipe pupils on eyes and fudge noses and mouths on muzzles (fig. 2).

Place the cookie sheet in the freezer for at least three hours before serving.

Note: These can be made up to a week in advance. Just place them in a covered container, or cover firmly frozen ice cream with plastic wrap.

Preparation time: 20 minutes
Freezing time: 3 hours or longer

Fig. 1

Fig. 2

PERDITA'S CHIPPER ICE-CREAM PUPS

D A L M A T I A N   C A K E

Miniature chocolate chips spot up the batter of this cake, while jumbo chocolate morsels dot the frosting. The effect is a spotted Dalmatian Cake, through and through.

Ingredients
2¼ cups flour
1⅔ cups sugar
⅔ cup shortening
1¼ cups milk
3½ tsp. baking powder
1 tsp. salt
1 tsp. almond extract
5 egg whites
1 6-oz. pkg. miniature semisweet chocolate chips
Almond Butter Frosting (recipe follows)
1 6-oz. pkg. extralarge semisweet chocolate chips or chunks
1 large white marshmallow
1 chocolate-covered bonbon
1 large red gumdrop

Directions
Combine the flour, sugar, shortening, milk, baking powder, salt, and almond extract in a large bowl. Blend the mixture until moistened, add egg whites, then beat with an electric mixer on high speed for two minutes longer. Fold in the miniature chocolate chips. Pour the batter into an 8″-round pan and an 8″-square pan that have both been lined with baking parchment. Bake in a preheated 350°F oven for thirty to thirty-five minutes or until a toothpick inserted in the center comes out clean. Cool the cakes completely, invert them from the pans, and peel the paper from the backs.

Cover a 16″-square piece of cardboard with foil. Cut the cakes according to figure 1 and arrange them on the board (fig. 2). Cover the cake smoothly with white frosting. Push a marshmallow in place for the eye and use the bonbon candy for the nose. Fill a small pastry bag, fitted with a #3 or #4 round writing tip, with black frosting. Dot the pupil on the eye and outline the cake as shown in figure 3 to define the paws, mouth, ears, etcetera. Arrange large chocolate chips at random for Dalmatian spots. Flatten the red gumdrop with a rolling pin and let it stick out of the side of the mouth to look like a tongue.

Note: This cake freezes well and may be made up to three weeks in advance, if it fits in the freezer. After the frosting has gotten firm for one hour, cover the cake tightly with plastic wrap, and place it back in the freezer.

DALMATIAN CAKE

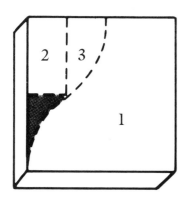

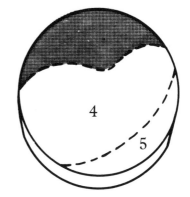

Fig. 1

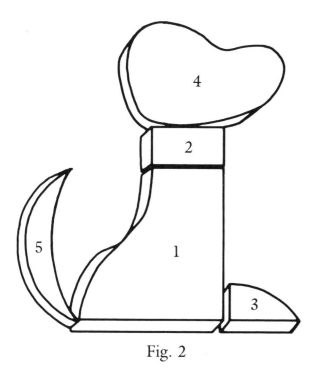

Fig. 2

Fig. 3

Almond Butter Frosting

Ingredients
¾ cup shortening
¾ cup butter or margarine, softened
1 tsp. almond extract
6 cups confectioners' sugar
4 tbs. milk
black gel food coloring

Directions
Cream the shortening, butter, and almond extract until smooth. Blend in the confectioners' sugar. Beat the mixture with enough milk to make a smooth spreading consistency. Set aside ¼ cup of frosting and tint it black.

Cake preparation time: 20 minutes
Baking time: 30 to 35 minutes
Frosting preparation and decoration time: 1 hour

P O L K A - D O T   M I L K

This vanilla-flavored milk is poured over frosty chocolate-chip ice cubes. It's a wonderful refreshment for small children.

Ingredients
1 gal. milk
1 tbs. vanilla extract
1 6-oz. bag miniature semisweet chocolate chips

Directions
Mix the vanilla into the milk. Divide the chocolate chips evenly among the cube sections of four ice cube trays. Pour the milk over the chips to fill and freeze trays for at least four hours. Meanwhile, chill the remaining milk. To serve, divide the ice among the serving cups and fill them with chilled milk.

   Note: This may be prepared up to three days in advance.

Preparation time: 10 minutes
Freezing time: 4 hours or longer

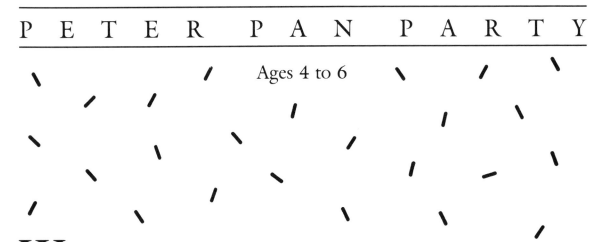

PETER PAN PARTY

Ages 4 to 6

Wendy Darling entertains her brothers, John and Michael, with tales about Peter Pan, an adventure-loving boy who lives in Never Land and refuses to grow up. To Wendy's father, Peter Pan is simply nonsensical make-believe, but to Wendy and the boys, he is very real, indeed. One night, Wendy's father forbids her to tell any more Peter Pan stories. That very night, while Wendy's parents are out, Peter Pan himself returns to the Darling household to retrieve the shadow he has left behind! Peter teaches the three children to fly and, with the fairy Tinker Bell, leads them off to Never Land, where they meet the Lost Boys, Tiger Lily, and the wicked Captain Hook.

Invitation: Map to Never Land

Decorations: Never Land Motif—map tablecloth; Crocodile Coin Clips; tepee napkins; pirate ship sails; skull-and-crossbones flag; ticking clock for sound effects

Get-acquainted Activity: Peter Pan Party Hats

Fantasy Feature: Crocodile Coin Clips

Games: Peter Pan's Shadow Hunt; Walk the Plank; Captain Hook's Treasure Chest

Menu: Cucumber Crocs (with Treasure Island Dip); Pirate Ship Poor Boys; Tiger Lily's Totem Pole Potatoes; Captain Hook's Ice-cream Heads; Crocodile Cake; Tinker Bell's Tangerine Punch

Map to Never Land

The invitation for the Peter Pan party comes with a map to Never Land—and pixie dust for flying there! Simply draw the map on a sheet of typing paper and make twelve copies.

Materials
black felt-tip pen
2 sheets typing paper
crayons
gold or silver glitter
12 letter-size mailing envelopes

Directions
Begin by drawing a map of Never Land (see page 48) on the first sheet of paper with a black felt-tip pen. Be sure to include Pirate's Cove, Crocodile Creek, Mermaid Lagoon, Skull Rock, Indian Camp, Misty Mountains, the Sea of Imagination, and Hangman's Tree.

On the second sheet of paper, write the following message:

This is your pass to
a Peter Pan Birthday Party

Sprinkle this pixie dust over
your head on (date), and fly to Never Land!
At (time) knock three times on Hangman's Tree at (your address)
and ask for (your child's name)
RSVP: (your phone number)

Make copies so that the map is on one side and the message is on the other side of the same sheet of paper. Use crayons to color each map. Fold the invitations, letter style, placing a teaspoon of glitter—Tinker Bell's pixie dust—in each one. Slip into envelopes and mail.

Preparation time: 45 minutes

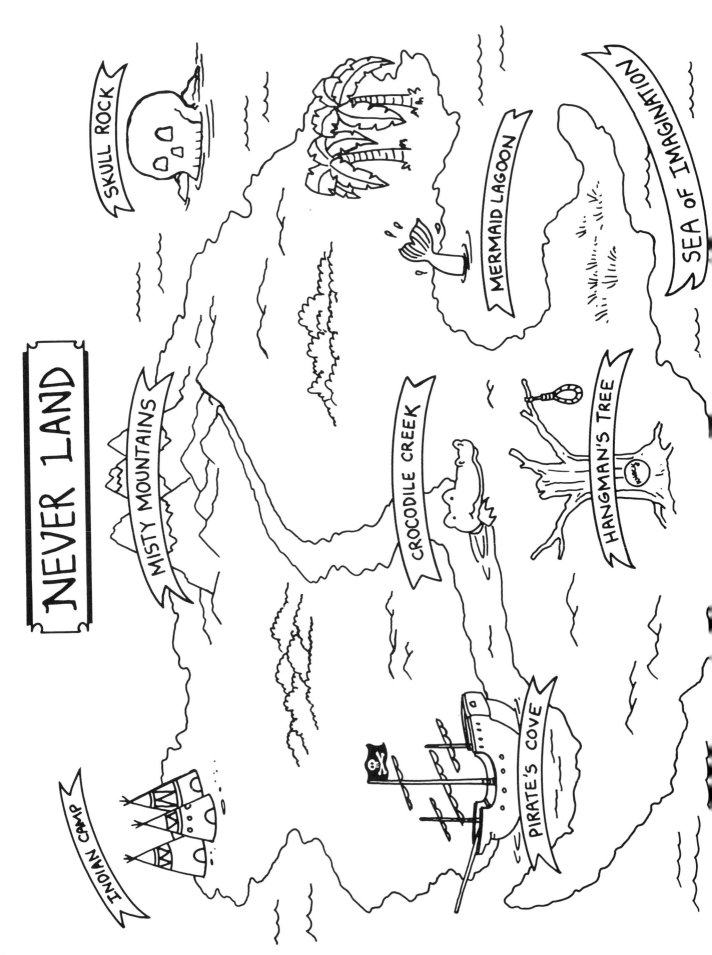

DECORATIONS

The decor for a Peter Pan party can be as eclectic as Never Land itself. From Pirate's Cove and the Indian Camp to Skull Rock and Hangman's Tree, there's certainly a wealth of possibilities! One way to incorporate all these themes is to use a map (like the one on the invitation) as a tablecloth. Draw Never Land on a large white paper tablecloth. Fill in the ocean (the Sea of Imagination) with blue crayon. Set out crayons on the table so that the children can color in the rest of the map. Crocodile Coin Clips can mark place settings, and the Crocodile Cake serves as the centerpiece. Fold paper napkins to look like Native American tepees, and decorate them with crayons. You can even rig pirate ship sails across the ceiling (or from a clothesline) using white sheets. And, of course, you've just got to make a black flag with a white skull and crossbones. Finally, add some sound effects for atmosphere. Remember how Captain Hook's old enemy, the Crocodile, swallowed a clock? Find a noisy windup clock, and hide it somewhere close by.

GET-ACQUAINTED ACTIVITY

Peter Pan Party Hats

Peter Pan dressed in green, from his pixie-pointed boots to his jaunty cap—except for the splash of red at the very top. Children can get into the Never Land spirit by making their own paper Peter Pan hats with bright red plumes.

Materials
12 20″ × 30″ sheets green tissue paper
stapler
12 red feathers (sold by the bag at craft and hobby shops)

Directions
Make up a sample hat, and set it on a craft table along with the paper, stapler, and feathers. As each child arrives, show him or her how to make the hat. First fold a sheet of tissue paper into a 20″ × 15″ rectangle, then into a 10″ × 15″ rectangle, with the main fold at the top. Fold down the corners of the top 7″ on each side (fig. 1). Fold up the bottom of each side 1″ and crease. Fold up another inch and crease again (fig. 2). Tuck one end under the other about 1½″ on each side, and staple in place (fig. 3). At one end of the hat, behind a fold, staple a red feather in place (fig. 4).

Preparation time: 5 minutes per hat

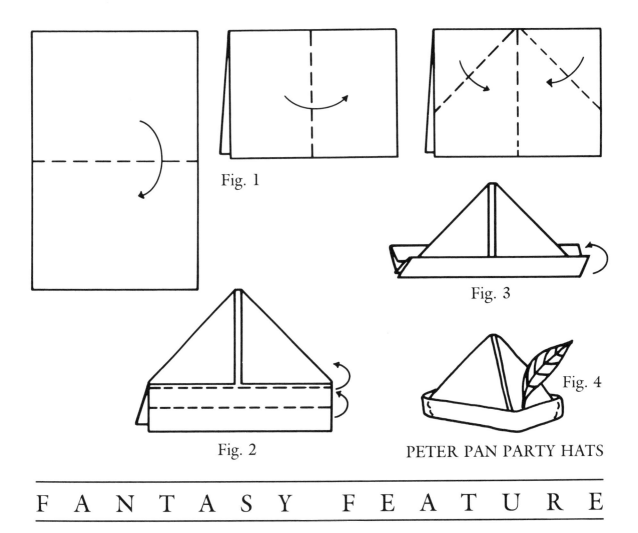

Fig. 1

Fig. 3

Fig. 2

Fig. 4

PETER PAN PARTY HATS

F A N T A S Y   F E A T U R E

Crocodile Coin Clips

The Crocodile Coin Clip is a clothespin contraption that makes a clever money clip, letter holder, potato chip bag clip, or even hair barrette. I like to use these crocs as place-card clips, each one grasping a child's name and a gold-foil-covered chocolate coin.

Materials
12 spring-action wooden clothespins
green felt-tip marker (wide chisel-tip)
black felt-tip pen (pen-point tip)
2 doz. glue-on hobby eyes, ⅜″ diameter
hobby glue (clear drying, super hold)
1 9″ × 12″ sheet green construction paper
scissors
pencil
ruler
12 gold-foil-covered chocolate coins

Directions

With the green felt-tip marker, color the entire exterior surface of the clothespins. (It's not necessary to color inside the mouth.) Glue an eye on each side of the pin, behind the large circular opening (fig. 1). With the black felt-tip pen, make two dots at the nose end of clothespin for nostrils. Cut the green paper into twelve 3″-square cards. Along the bottom of each card, write the name of one guest and clip it, with a gold coin, between the jaws of a crocodile(fig. 2). Use as place markers.

Preparation time: 30 minutes

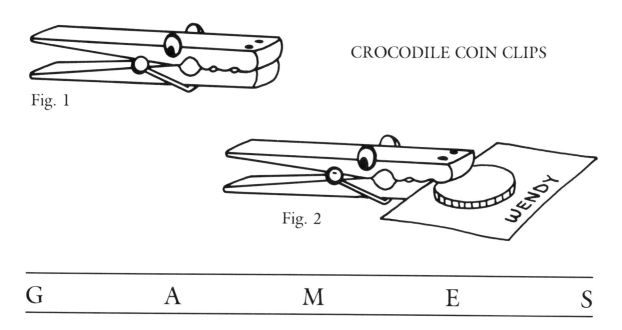

CROCODILE COIN CLIPS

Fig. 1

Fig. 2

G　　　A　　　M　　　E　　　S

Peter Pan's Shadow Hunt

Peter Pan first met Wendy and her brothers when he visited the nursery in search of his missing shadow. Wendy's first act of friendship was to sew Peter's shadow back on for him.

For this game you'll need twelve sheets of black tissue paper. Cut the silhouette figure of a boy out of one sheet. Crumple it into a wad. Crumple the other eleven sheets of tissue paper as well. Hide all twelve sheets in various places around the house or yard. Children must go in search of the shadow, and the one who brings it back is the winner.

Walk the Plank

Captain Hook's band of pirates hid near Hangman's Tree in hopes of capturing Peter Pan. Instead, they kidnapped Wendy, Michael, John, and the Lost Boys and brought them all back to Hook's ship. There Captain Hook ordered his prisoners to join the crew . . . or walk the plank!

This game is basically a balance test. You'll need a sturdy, straight (not warped) 6′-

long two-by-four for a plank and two bricks or concrete blocks. Prop the board up at each end with a brick so that the 4″ side is parallel to the ground. (The plank should stand only about 2″ to 3″ above the ground.) Children pretend that they are Captain Hook's captives and line up at one end of the plank. Pass out twelve wide, loose-fitting rubber bands for the children to bind their wrists together behind their backs. The players take turns walking across the plank, trying not to lose their balance and step off. As each child finishes, he or she goes back to the end of the line for another round. Any player who doesn't make it across is "eaten by the Crocodile"—in other words, is out. Eventually, almost everyone will end up overboard. The last remaining player is the prize-winning plank-walker.

Captain Hook's Treasure Chest

Fishing for favors is a time-honored party activity. Usually it's done with fishing rods. This game is a slight variation on the theme. First you'll need to make a treasure chest by decorating a large cardboard box. (If you already have some kind of trunk, so much the better!) Fill the chest with candy and/or favors that have been wrapped in colored tissue with a ribbon loop on each. For Captain Hook's hook use a coat hanger. Bend the hanger so that there's a handle for holding the hook.

Kids take turns being blindfolded and reaching into the chest with the hook to get a prize. If the hook snares more than one favor, the extra favors must be thrown back.

Menu

C U C U M B E R   C R O C S

(with Treasure Island Dip)

12 servings

Carving cucumbers into crocodiles is similar to soap sculpting, only in this case the art-work is edible. The crocodiles are actually very easy to prepare—but it helps to practice on a couple of spare cucumbers. Serve them on lunch plates along with little cups filled with Treasure Island Dip.

Ingredients
6 whole cucumbers (the longer, the better)
Treasure Island Dip (recipe follows)

PETER PAN PARTY—Pirate Ship Poor Boys (p. 54)

Directions

Wash wax off the cucumbers. Split each cucumber in half, lengthwise, and scoop out the seeds. Use a small, narrow paring knife that's easy to manipulate. Cut each cucumber in half according to the top view in figure 1 and the side view in figure 2. (You might want to draw the outline of a crocodile on each cucumber half using a nontoxic watercolor marker.) To score scales on the back and to cut eyes and nostrils into the head (fig. 3), use a linoleum knife or the tip of a vegetable parer. Serve the crocodiles with individual cups of Treasure Island Dip.

Note: Cucumbers may be prepared in advance and stored in the refrigerator, covered with plastic wrap.

CUCUMBER CROCS

Fig. 1

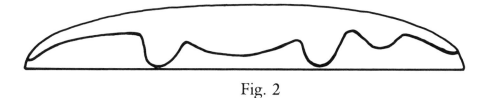

Fig. 2

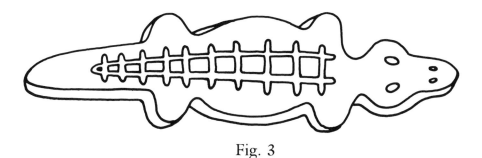

Fig. 3

Treasure Island Dip (similar to Thousand Island dressing)

Ingredients
1 cup regular or nonfat mayonnaise
1 tbs. minced celery
2 tbs. minced green or red bell pepper
1 tbs. sweet pickle relish
¼ cup chili sauce
1 hard-boiled egg, chopped
½ tsp. salt
½ tsp. onion powder

Directions
Combine the ingredients in a mixing bowl until blended. Chill at least two hours before serving.
  Note: Dressing may be prepared up to three days in advance.

Preparation time: 30 minutes
Chilling time: 2 hours or longer

PIRATE SHIP POOR BOYS

12 servings

With paper sails, carrot curl flags, and olive portholes, these poor boys make very convincing pirate ships. . . . Good enough even for Captain Hook!

Ingredients
6 hero, or grinder, rolls (6″ to 8″ long)
⅓ cup mild mustard
4 doz. black olives
4 doz. thin pretzel sticks
12 lettuce leaves (green or red leaf)
⅔ cup regular or nonfat mayonnaise
2 lbs. deli-sliced ham or turkey (extra thin)
12 9″ wooden skewers or strong, thin plastic straws
12 paper pirate sails (instructions follow)
12 carrot flags (instructions follow)
white paint

Directions

Split rolls in half, lengthwise, and spread with mustard. Make a slit in the closed end of each olive, and insert one end of a pretzel stick into the slit. Each pretzel stick should have two olives on it (fig. 1). Line up four pretzel sticks with olives on each roll for portholes (fig. 2). Place lettuce leaves on top of each roll, and spread with mayonnaise. Arrange the deli slices in a folded fashion on top of the lettuce. Insert skewers through the paper pirate sails to make billowing sails, and add an olive crow's nest near the top of each skewer. Stick a carrot flag on the tip, and insert one skewer in the center of each sandwich (fig. 3).

To make carrot flags, cut thin slices, lengthwise, from peeled carrots. Cut one end to a point to resemble a flag. Soak in ice water for several hours (or overnight) until pieces become slightly wavy. To make pirate sails, cut twelve sails from black construction paper (6½″ × 3½″ at the base—tapering to 2½″ at the top). Paint skull and crossbones with white paint on sails.

Preparation time: 25 minutes

PIRATE SHIP
POOR BOYS

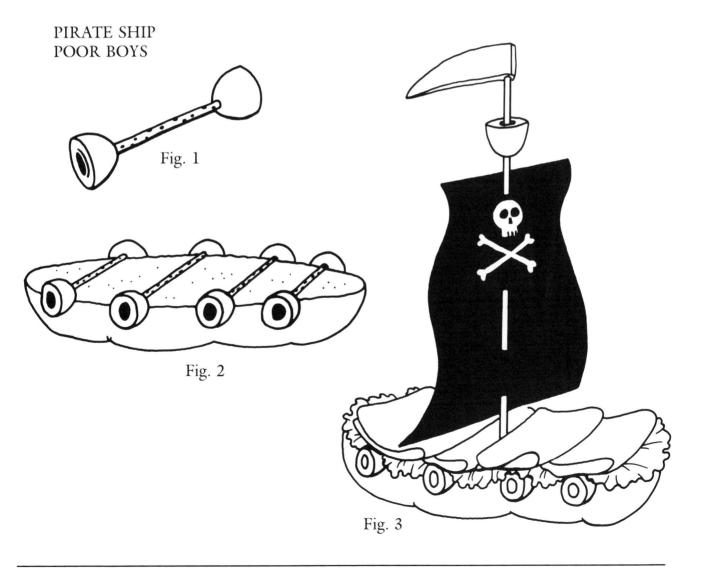

Fig. 1

Fig. 2

Fig. 3

TIGER LILY'S TOTEM POLE POTATOES

12 servings

Like baked potatoes on a stick, red-skinned new potatoes are skewered and roasted in the oven. Fierce or funny faces are carved into each potato, and the potatoes, stacked on skewers, resemble Indian totem poles.

Ingredients

4 to 5 doz. red-skinned new potatoes
12 wooden skewers
1 to 2 tbs. olive oil
1 cup sour cream with chives
1 cup whipped butter

Directions

Wash and scrub the potatoes. Using a paring knife, carve faces into the potatoes. Try to vary the expressions. Pieces of the potatoes can be cut away to form ears, nose, and so on (fig. 1). Skewer four to five potatoes on each stick (fig. 2), and brush with olive oil. Bake in a preheated 375°F oven for forty-five minutes, turning once. Serve warm with the Pirate Ship Poor Boys. Set out crocks of sour cream and butter on the table for children to use as toppings.

 Note: These are best when carved and baked the day of the party.

Preparation time: 30 minutes
Baking time: 45 minutes

TIGER LILY'S TOTEM POLE POTATOES

Fig. 1

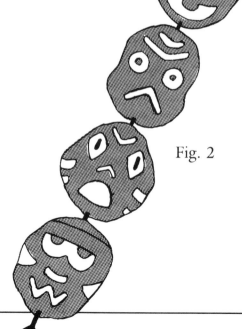

Fig. 2

CAPTAIN HOOK'S ICE-CREAM HEADS

12 servings

Ingredients

½ gal. French vanilla ice cream
3 doz. whole, blanched almonds
12 marshmallows
3 Maraschino cherries, quartered
1½ cups fudge sauce (any brand that becomes thickened and firm when frozen)
12 1½-oz. chocolate peppermint patties
2 pkgs. fruit rolls
12 small gold candy balls (used in food decoration)

Directions

To prepare fruit roll feathers, cut red or yellow fruit-roll candy into twelve 3″ × ¾″ pieces. Trim ends of rectangles into points, and cut gashes into sides for feathered look. Prepare Captain Hook's hats by cutting each mint patty in half, placing a fruit-roll feather in between the halves, and sandwiching the halves together (back to back) with a dot of fudge sauce (fig. 1). Then cover a baking sheet with foil. Working quickly, place twelve large round ice-cream scoops on the foil, evenly spaced. Press an almond with the small end pointing up into the front of each scoop for a nose. Press another almond with the small end pointing down into the sides of each scoop for ears. Push one marshmallow into each scoop, on the upper-left-hand side of the nose. Press a slice of cherry ½″ underneath the nose for a mouth (fig. 2). Fill a small pastry bag, fitted with a #2 small round writing tip, with fudge sauce. Pipe a pupil onto each eye, and make an eye patch where the second eye would be. Pipe a strap for the eye patch and a mustache under the nose. Pipe squiggly lines near the top for curly hair. Sit a mint hat on top of each scoop, and press a gold ball under one ear of each scoop for an earring (fig. 3). Freeze at least three hours before serving.

Note: These can be made up to three days in advance and stored in the freezer, either firmly covered with plastic wrap or in a covered container.

Preparation time: 20 minutes
Freezing time: 3 hours or longer

Fig. 1

Fig. 2

Fig. 3

CAPTAIN HOOK'S ICE-CREAM HEADS

C R O C O D I L E   C A K E

12 servings

Pineapple and coconut add a tropical taste to this luscious lizard.

Ingredients
1 20-oz. can crushed pineapple, with juice
2 cups sugar
2 cups flour
2 tsp. baking soda
2 eggs
½ cup vegetable oil
½ tsp. coconut extract
1 cup shredded coconut
Vanilla Buttercream Frosting (recipe follows)
2 large marshmallows

Directions
Combine pineapple and juice with sugar, flour, baking soda, eggs, oil, extract, and coconut in mixing bowl. Beat on medium speed for two minutes. Pour into an 8″-square cake pan and an 8″-round cake pan, both lined with baking parchment. Bake in a preheated 350°F oven for twenty-five to thirty minutes or until a toothpick inserted in the center of each cake comes out clean.

Cover a 26″ × 10″ piece of cardboard with foil. Cut the cakes according to figure 1, and rearrange the pieces according to figure 2. Cover the cake with green frosting, and place marshmallows on the head for eyes (fig. 3). Fill a pastry bag, fitted with a coupling nozzle, with the remaining green frosting. Attach a #5 star tip, and pipe ridges from the base of Crocodile's head to the tip of its tail. Remove the star tip, and attach a #6 round writing tip. Build up frosting behind the marshmallow eyes, and make loops for nostrils. Pipe toes at the base of the feet. Fill a small pastry bag, fitted with a #2 small round writing tip, with black frosting. Pipe pupils onto the eyes, and add a grinning mouth (fig. 4).

Note: The large size and shape of this cake make it awkward to freeze. It's best prepared no more than two days in advance.

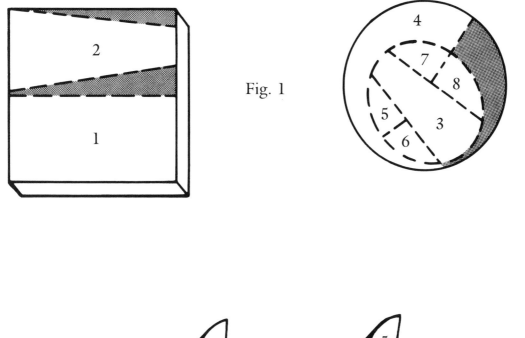

Fig. 1

Fig. 2

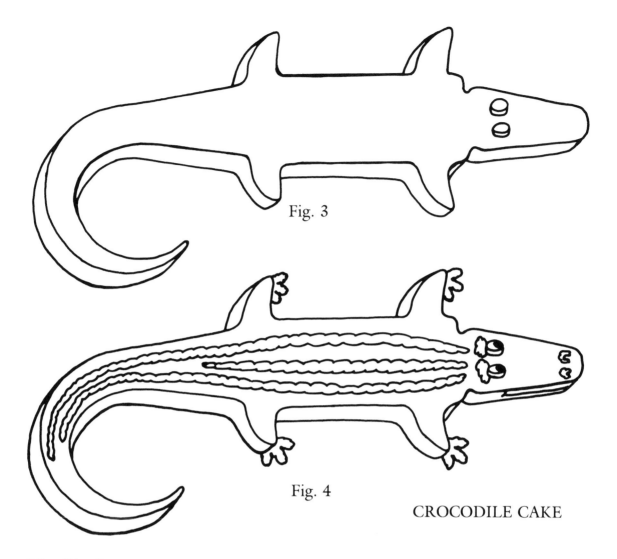

Fig. 3

Fig. 4

CROCODILE CAKE

Vanilla Buttercream Frosting

Ingredients
1 cup butter or margarine, softened
2 tsp. vanilla extract
8 cups confectioners' sugar
5 to 7 tbs. milk
green and black gel food coloring

Directions
Cream butter and vanilla until light and fluffy. Beat in sugar and enough milk to make frosting smooth and spreadable. Remove 3 tbs. of frosting, and tint black. Tint the remaining frosting green.

Preparation time: 1 hour
Baking time: 25 to 30 minutes

TINKER BELL'S TANGERINE PUNCH

12+ servings

Ingredients
1 15-oz. can mandarin orange segments, drained
3 qts. lemonade
½ gal. tangerine (or orange) juice
⅓ cup grenadine syrup

Directions
Drain the orange segments, and divide them among four ice cube trays. Fill the trays with lemonade, and freeze for at least five hours. Mix the remaining lemonade with the tangerine juice and the grenadine syrup. Chill until serving time. To serve, divide the ice among the cups, and fill the cups with punch.

Preparation time: 10 minutes
Freezing time: 5 hours or longer

THE JUNGLE BOOK PARTY

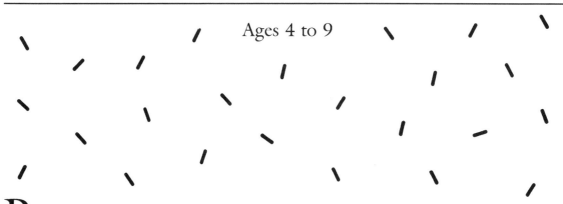

Ages 4 to 9

Based on a work by Rudyard Kipling, *The Jungle Book* film is the saga of Mowgli, a Man-cub left abandoned in the jungle and raised by a family of wolves. When the sinister tiger Shere Khan returns to the wolves' part of the jungle, it is no longer safe for Mowgli to remain there. But Mowgli is undaunted by the threat of Shere Khan and would rather stay in the jungle with his friends than go live in the Man-village. He decides to leave the jungle only when he spots a creature he has never before seen . . . a young girl.

Invitation: Panther Paw

Decorations: Jungle Motif—ferns; leafy greens; fresh tropical fruits

Get-acquainted Activity: Popcorn Pythons

Fantasy Feature: Krispy Shere Khan

Games: Elephant March; King Louie's Banana Dance; The Coconut Bowl

Menu: Bagheera's Banana Ambrosia; Baloo's Burgers (with Safari Sauce); Tiger Taters; Kaa's Kake; Mowgli's Mocha Monkeys; Jungle Juice

Panther Paw

If anyone knows the way around the jungle, it is Bagheera the panther. This invitation is a panther paw, guiding guests to a Jungle Book party.

Materials
12 9″ × 12″ sheets black construction paper
6 9″ × 12″ sheets green construction paper
tracing paper
pencil
scissors
1 sheet thin poster board
rubber cement
black felt-tip marker
gray poster or acrylic paint
stapler
12 5″ × 7″ envelopes

Directions
With tracing paper and pencil, trace the paw patterns on page 65. Cut out the tracings, and then, using rubber cement, glue them to a sheet of thin poster board and cut out two paw stencils. Using the panther paw stencil, draw twenty-four paws onto the black construction paper, and cut them out. Draw twelve message paws onto the green construction paper and cut them out. On each green paw, write the following message with the black marker:

The path of the panther paw
leads to
THE JUNGLE BOOK PARTY
for Man-cub (your child's name)
Follow my footprint to (your address)
on (date) at (time)
RSVP (your phone number)

On twelve of the black paper paws, paint paw pads and claws with gray paint. Allow the paint to dry. Use these as the top sheets of the invitations. Sandwich the green message sheets between a top sheet and a bottom black paw, and staple through all three layers at the bottom (fig. 1). Mail them in envelopes that have been decorated with panther paw prints (fig. 2).

Preparation time: 1 hour

PANTHER PAW INVITATION

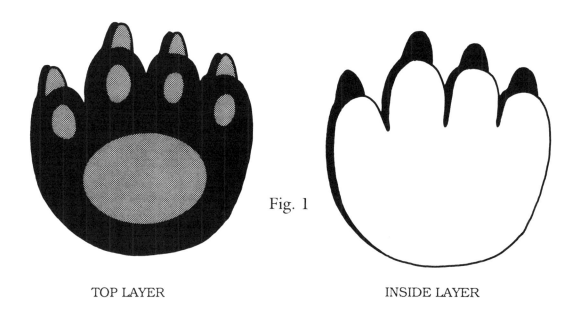

Fig. 1

TOP LAYER   INSIDE LAYER

Fig. 2

PANTHER PAW INVITATION

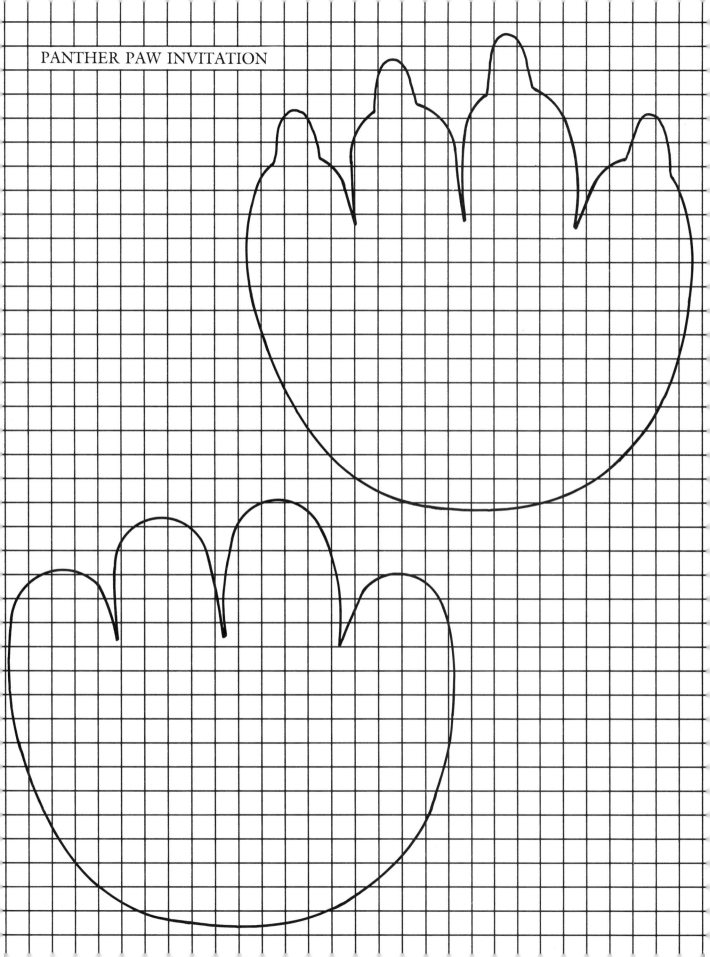

D E C O R A T I O N S

A jungle party calls for a tropical touch. You can actually find most of the decorations you'll need in the produce department of your supermarket. For jungle ferns and other flora, look for a variety of leafy greens, such as spinach, kale, sorrel, basil, arugula, and beet greens. Arrange these on a table covered with a green paper cloth, and add an abundance of fresh tropical fruits: pineapples, coconuts, kiwifruits, and cascades of bananas. Make room down the center of the table for the star attraction, Kaa's Kake, a four-foot-long peanut butter python!

G E T - A C Q U A I N T E D   A C T I V I T Y

Popcorn Pythons

Candied popcorn is wrapped in clear plastic to make a slinky snake. This python even has a red ribbon tongue!

Materials
1 roll yellow and 1 roll green plastic wrap
8 qts. popcorn (caramel, green apple, or any variety of flavors
from a popcorn shop)
curling ribbon (green, yellow, and red)
6 9″ × 12″ sheets construction paper, yellow and green; 3 of each color
1 8″ × 11″ sheet white paper
glue
scissors
black felt-tip marker

Directions
For this activity you'll want to have bowls of assorted popcorn set out on a table along with the craft materials. (It's a good idea to precut the python heads from the construction paper according to the pattern on page 68 and to have a sample snake already made up.) For each python, tear off 2½″ of plastic wrap. Show children how to place about ¼ cup of popcorn at 4″ intervals down the length of the plastic wrap (fig. 1), leaving about 6″ at each end. Roll up the plastic in a tube around the popcorn (fig. 2). Tie off into sections using short pieces of ribbon in a color that contrasts with the plastic wrap (fig. 3). Fold the paper head along the crease lines. Pull one end of the plastic wrap through the slash in the crease. Tie a knot in the plastic wrap so it won't slip back through the slash (fig. 4). Tie a 12″ strand of red ribbon around the knot in the mouth for a tongue. Cut out eyes from white paper, glue them on, and draw eyes and nostrils on the head with a marker (fig. 5).

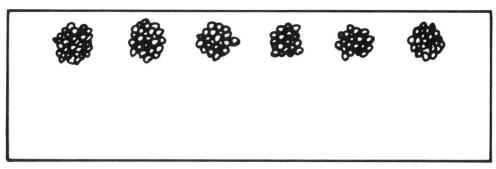

Fig. 1

Fig. 2

Fig. 3

Fig. 4

Fig. 5

POPCORN PYTHONS

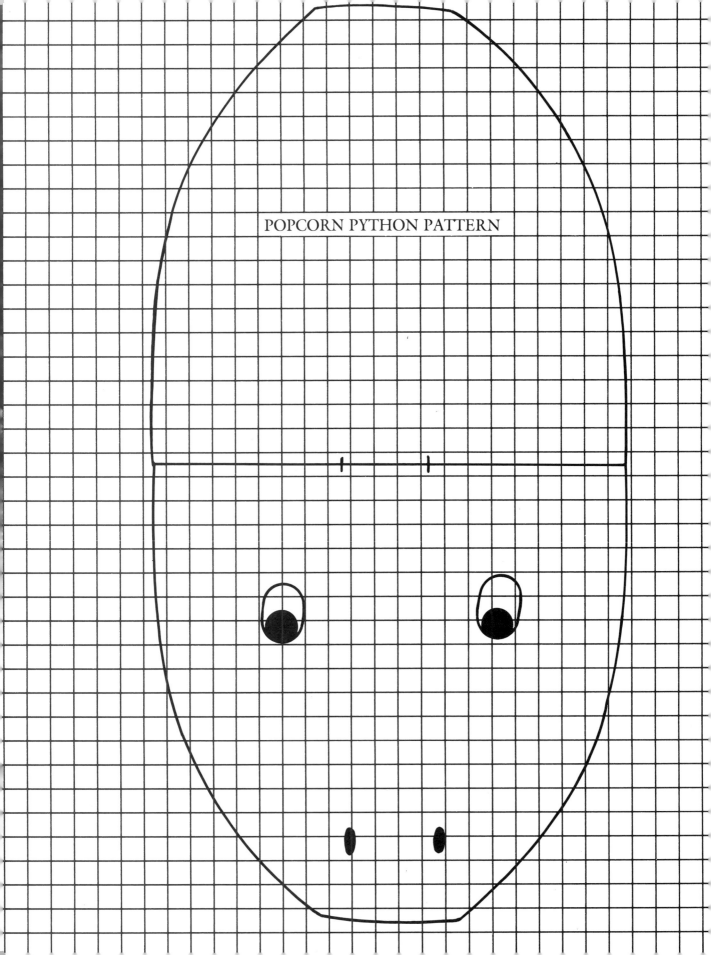

POPCORN PYTHON PATTERN

THE JUNGLE BOOK PARTY — Popcorn Python (p. 66) and Krispy Shere Khan (p. 69)

Krispy Shere Khan

These crisp cereal tigers will remind you of popcorn balls. Use them to decorate each child's place setting.

Ingredients
2 cups butter or margarine
orange gel food coloring (or a mixture of yellow and red)
6 cups miniature marshmallows
12 cups toasted rice cereal
2 doz. large orange gumdrops
2 doz. additional miniature marshmallows
1 doz. large black licorice gumdrops
Chocolate Stripes (recipe and instructions follow)

Directions
Melt the butter in a very large saucepan, and add the 6 cups of miniature marshmallows. Stir over a low heat until the marshmallows are melted and the mixture is smooth. Tint the mixture bright orange with the food coloring. Remove the pan from the heat, and add the cereal, gently stirring until it's evenly coated. Allow to cool for about three minutes. With buttered hands, divide the mixture into a dozen egg-shaped balls (fig. 1). Flatten the orange gumdrops with your fingers, and press one onto each side of the end of an oval for ears. Press two miniature marshmallows into each head for eyes, and press a black gumdrop into the small end of each head for the nose (fig. 2). Using a clean, narrow-pointed paintbrush, apply Chocolate Stripes along the sides of the cheeks and on top of each head. Paint pupils on the eyes and a mouth under each nose (fig. 3). Place the tiger heads on a foil-covered baking sheet, and chill them in the refrigerator until the cereal and chocolate are firm.

Note: These can be made up to three days in advance and stored at room temperature. They can be stored in the refrigerator for several weeks. If you don't have a very large saucepan and mixing bowl to work with, consider making this recipe in two batches.

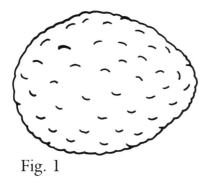

Fig. 1

Fig. 2

Fig. 3

Chocolate Stripes

Ingredients
1 6-oz. bag semisweet chocolate chips
2 tbs. shortening

Directions
Melt the chips and shortening in the top of a double boiler (or in a microwave). Stir until smooth.

Preparation time: 45 minutes
Chilling time: 30 minutes or longer

Elephant March

"Hup! Two! Three! Four!" In *The Jungle Book,* Mowgli encounters the Dawn Patrol—a parading troop of pachyderms headed by Colonel Hathi. The big elephant shouts commands to the other elephants in seemingly endless military drills through the jungle. "Order in the ranks!" or "Dress up that line!" Hathi would shout at one elephant or another.

In this game, which resembles Simon Says, one child is appointed to play Colonel Hathi and is issued a whistle. The other children fall in line and form a troop of elephants. The elephants march in place or in a line while Hathi gives orders and chants, "Hup! Two! Three! Four!" Hathi blows his or her whistle and then gives a command. If Hathi gives an order without blowing the whistle first, it's not to be considered an official order. As in Simon Says, such order should be ignored. If an elephant accidentally follows an unofficial order, he or she is out of the ranks. The last elephant left in the troop gets to play Colonel Hathi in the next military drill.

Here are some orders that Colonel Hathi might use: "Company halt!" (elephants stop); "Attention!" (elephants salute); "Company left face!" (elephants turn left); "Company right face!" (elephants turn right); "Company about-face!" (elephants turn around).

King Louie's Banana Dance

King Louie, the swinging, scat-singing monkey monarch, loves to dance!

In this activity, children have an opportunity to make up a funny dance, with each child contributing one step. Dancers line up side by side across the yard or a large room. Starting from left to right, each child steps in front of the line and makes up any silly step that comes to mind. The dance is built by a progressive series of steps, with a rehearsal after each stage of development. Naturally, the dance grows more and more complex with each player's input. The real challenge is the grand finale, when everyone tries to remember what step comes next. For musical accompaniment, you can use the tape from *The Jungle Book* or from any of your child's favorite songs.

The Coconut Bowl

For bowling "jungle style," use pineapples for the pins and a coconut for the ball! The secret is to select tall pineapples—fat, squat pineapples won't tip over. Three or four pineapples will work just fine, along with a nice round coconut. Line the pineapples up about 8″ apart on a smooth floor or surface. The bowling alley need be only about 12′ long. The players take turns trying to knock down a pineapple with the coconut. Knocking down one pineapple is a strike, and every strike gets a second shot. Keep score. The player with the most strikes wins.

Menu

BAGHEERA'S BANANA AMBROSIA

12 servings

This pineapple-and-orange ambrosia is enhanced by the addition of kiwifruits and bananas. A touch of cinnamon adds a new taste twist.

Ingredients
2 15-oz. cans mandarin orange segments, drained
1 fresh pineapple, peeled, cored, and cubed
4 kiwifruits, peeled and sliced
4 bananas, peeled and sliced
1 cup shredded coconut
1 tbs. lime juice
2 tbs. honey
1 tbs. sugar
1 tsp. cinnamon

Directions
Combine the fruit in a large bowl. In a separate cup, blend the lime juice, honey, sugar, and cinnamon. Pour it over the fruit and gently toss with half of the coconut. Chill for two hours before serving. Spoon into individual serving dishes and sprinkle with the remaining coconut.
Note: This should be prepared the same day as the party for optimum freshness.

Preparation time: 15 minutes
Chilling time: 2 hours

BALOO'S BURGERS

(with Safari Sauce)

12+ servings

Top these hamburgers off with a Bear Bun and some zesty Safari Sauce. The Bear Buns are simple to make, using canned, refrigerated bread sticks. The Safari Sauce adds the zesty zing of chutney to an already delicious topping. This recipe yields sixteen bread heads, so you can cook some extra hamburger patties for hearty appetites.

Ingredients

3 cans (8 count) soft bread sticks
1 egg, beaten with 1 tbs. water
3 doz. raisins
12–16 3-oz. hamburger patties
condiments: lettuce, tomato slices, pickles, mustard, catsup, and Safari Sauce (recipe follows)

Directions

Open two cans of bread sticks and separate them along the perforations (do not unroll them). Place the rolls 4″ apart on two baking pans sprayed with nonstick cooking spray. Flatten the coiled buns slightly (fig. 1). Open the remaining can, unroll the bread sticks, and cut each bread stick into 6 equal pieces. (It will take three pieces to form the ears and nose on each bun.) Roll each of the pieces into a small pinwheel (fig. 2). Press two pieces *firmly* on both sides of the top edge of each bun for ears and one in the center for a snout (fig. 3). Brush with egg. Push three raisins *firmly* in place for the eyes and the nose on each bun (fig. 4).

Bake in a preheated 350°F oven for fifteen to eighteen minutes or until golden brown. After they've cooled, *carefully* split the buns open with a serrated bread knife (avoid breaking off the ears). Just before serving, grill or charcoal broil hamburger patties and serve them on the buns with assorted condiments (fig. 5).

Note: Bread may be baked and prepared the day before, then stored in plastic bags.

Safari Sauce

Ingredients

1 cup regular or nonfat mayonnaise
⅔ cup catsup
¼ cup chopped mango chutney (may substitute with sweet pickle relish)
½ tsp. dry mustard

Directions

Combine the ingredients in a small mixing bowl and blend until smooth. Chill until serving time.

Preparation time: 25 minutes
Baking time: 15 to 18 minutes

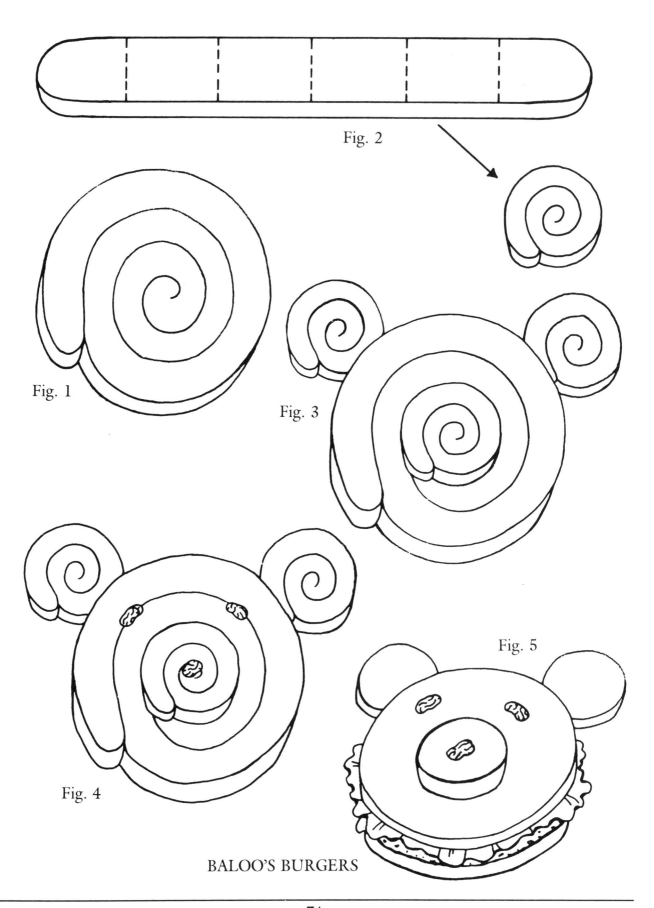

Fig. 2

Fig. 1

Fig. 3

Fig. 5

Fig. 4

BALOO'S BURGERS

T I G E R T A T E R S

Ordinary tater tots become a roaring new taste sensation with a sprinkling of sesame seeds and a hint of curry. (The curry powder adds that special East Indian accent.) Don't worry about picky eaters; there's no such thing as an exotic french fry! These are willingly wolfed down.

Ingredients
1 32-oz. bag frozen potato puffs
¼ cup sesame oil
1 tbs. curry powder
½ tsp. salt
¼ cup sesame seeds

Directions
Put the frozen potatoes in a large mixing or salad bowl. In a separate bowl, stir the curry powder and salt into the oil. Pour the mixture over the potatoes and sprinkle in the sesame seeds. Gently toss until the potatoes are evenly coated. Spread them into two jelly-roll pans and bake in a preheated 400°F oven for about twenty minutes (shaking to turn, while baking) until golden and crisp. Transfer the potatoes to paper towels to drain off any excess oil. Serve them warm.

Note: These can be baked in two batches if your oven is small. They can also be held in a warm oven for about an hour.

Preparation time: 5 minutes
Baking time: 20 minutes

K A A ' S K A K E

12 + servings

Kids will squeal with delight when they see a slinky four-foot snake cake in the center of the table. Kaa, the python, is created simply by cutting and rearranging peanut butter pound cakes.

Ingredients
3 cups flour
1½ cups firmly packed brown sugar
½ cup butter or margarine, softened
⅓ cup creamy peanut butter
1½ cups milk
4½ tsp. baking powder
1 tsp. salt
1 tsp. vanilla extract
3 eggs
Peanut Butter Frosting (recipe follows)
Chocolate Stripes (recipe follows)
1 large marshmallow
1 red licorice lace

Directions
Combine the flour, sugar, butter, peanut butter, milk, baking powder, salt, vanilla, and eggs in a large mixing bowl, and blend until moistened. Beat the mixture for three minutes at a high speed with an electric mixer. Divide the batter evenly among three 8″-round pans lined with baking parchment. Bake the cakes in a preheated 350°F oven for thirty to thirty-five minutes or until a toothpick inserted into the center of the cakes comes out clean.

Cool the cakes completely. Invert them from the pans and peel the parchment paper from the bottoms. Cover a 5′-long, 10″-wide piece of cardboard with foil. Cut the cakes according to the diagrams in figure 1, and arrange the pieces on the cake board as shown in figure 2. Prepare the Peanut Butter Frosting and the Chocolate Stripes. Cover the entire cake with Peanut Butter Frosting. Fill a medium-sized pastry bag, fitted with a #5 medium round writing tip, with chocolate frosting. Pipe stripes on the python. Flatten the marshmallow slightly and use it for an eye. Pipe a pupil on the eye. Insert a doubled strand of red licorice in the mouth for a tongue (fig. 3).

Note: Because of this cake's size, it's not practical for freezing. It's best to prepare it not more than two days in advance.

Peanut Butter Frosting

Ingredients
8 cups confectioners' sugar
⅔ cup creamy peanut butter
⅔ cup butter or margarine, softened
½ to ⅔ cup milk

Directions
Beat ingredients with an electric mixer until the frosting is smooth and of spreading consistency. If necessary, beat in additional milk, a little at a time.

Chocolate Stripes

Ingredients
2 cups confectioners' sugar
¼ cup cocoa
¼ cup butter or margarine, softened
1 tsp. vanilla extract
2 to 3 tbs. milk

Directions
Beat all of the ingredients until smooth and creamy, adding additional milk if needed.

Preparation time: 1 hour
Baking time: 30 to 35 minutes

KAA'S KAKE

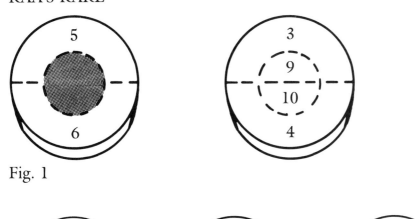

Fig. 1

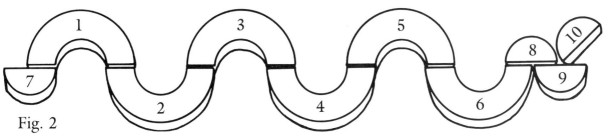

Fig. 2

Fig. 3

M O W G L I ' S   M O C H A   M O N K E Y S

12 servings

Ingredients
½-gal. coffee (or chocolate) ice cream
24 miniature marshmallows
1½ cups fudge sauce (any brand that becomes thickened and firm when frozen)
2 doz. pecan halves

Directions
Cover a baking dish with aluminum foil. Place twelve large, round scoops of ice cream on the foil, about 3″ apart. Push miniscoops of ice cream into the large scoops at the base for faces. Push two marshmallows into the large scoops for eyes (fig. 1). Fill a small pastry bag, fitted with a #3 or #4 small round writing tip, with fudge sauce. Pipe pupils on the eyes. Pipe a mouth and nostrils on each small ice-cream scoop. Pipe long shaggy monkey fur around each monkey head, and insert pecan halves on each side for ears (fig. 2).

Return the monkeys to the freezer for at least three hours before serving.

Note: These can be made up to a week in advance if stored in a covered container or covered firmly with plastic wrap.

Preparation time: 20 minutes
Freezing time: 3 hours or longer

Fig. 1

Fig. 2

MOWGLI'S MOCHA MONKEYS

J U N G L E   J U I C E

This green pineapple punch looks even more exotic with a kiwifruit slice served on the edge of each cup.

Ingredients
½ gal. pineapple juice
½ gal. limeade (ready to serve or frozen, prepared)
4 kiwifruits

Directions
Combine the pineapple juice and the limeade. Fill about four ice cube trays with punch and freeze them for at least five hours. Meanwhile, chill the remaining punch. To serve, divide the ice among the cups and pour the punch over the ice. Cut the ends off the kiwifruits and cut about three thick, round slices from each fruit. Cut a notch halfway through the diameter of each slice and slip one onto the edge of each cup or glass.

   Note: Punch and ice may be prepared up to three days in advance.

Preparation time: 15 minutes
Freezing time: 5 hours or longer

THE LITTLE MERMAID PARTY

The little mermaid Ariel lives under the sea along with a host of colorful characters, including her father, King Triton; her best friend, Flounder; and Sebastian, the singing crab. But Ariel longs to be part of the human world, and one night, when she spots the handsome human Prince Eric, she falls in love with him at once. In order to win his heart, Ariel enlists the help of Ursula, the evil Sea Witch, but Ursula has a wicked plan to snare Eric for herself. In the end, it's Prince Eric to the rescue, and King Triton, in gratitude, grants his daughter her dearest wish: to become human and marry the prince.

Invitation: Scallop Shell

Decorations: Caribbean Sea Motif: fishnets; seashells; coral; fishbowl with a goldfish

Get-acquainted Activity: King Triton's Shell Shop

Fantasy Feature: Ariel's Treasure Chest with Dinglehoppers and Bubble-blowing Snarfblats

Games: Mermaid Marathon, Starfish Fishing; Loony Limbo

Menu: Flounder's Fruit Salad; Under-the-Sea Biscuits; Seaweed Slaw; Guppy Cups; Ursula's Sea Witch Sherbert; Sebastian's Crab Cakes; Caribbean Blue Cooler

Scallop Shell

Marbleized wrapping paper in pastel shades makes a lovely cover for this invitation. You can also use pale, pearlized paper that has a luminous quality similar to a seashell.

Materials
13 9″ × 12″ sheets white poster board
tracing paper
rubber cement
1 pkg. or roll marbleized or pearlized gift wrap
4 yds. pastel or iridescent pearlized ribbon
scissors
pencils
pink felt-tip marker
stapler
12 9″ × 12″ white envelopes

Directions
With tracing paper and pencil, trace the scallop shell pattern on page 82. Cut out the tracing and glue it to one sheet of the poster board. Cut this out and use it as a stencil for cutting twelve shells each from the poster board and from the gift wrap. Decorate the poster board along its edges with pink marker to form a border (fig. 1). In the center of each poster board shell, write the following message:

Ariel invites you under the sea
to
a party among the Merpeople
for
(your child's name)'s birthday
on (date) at (time)
(your address)
RSVP: (your phone number)

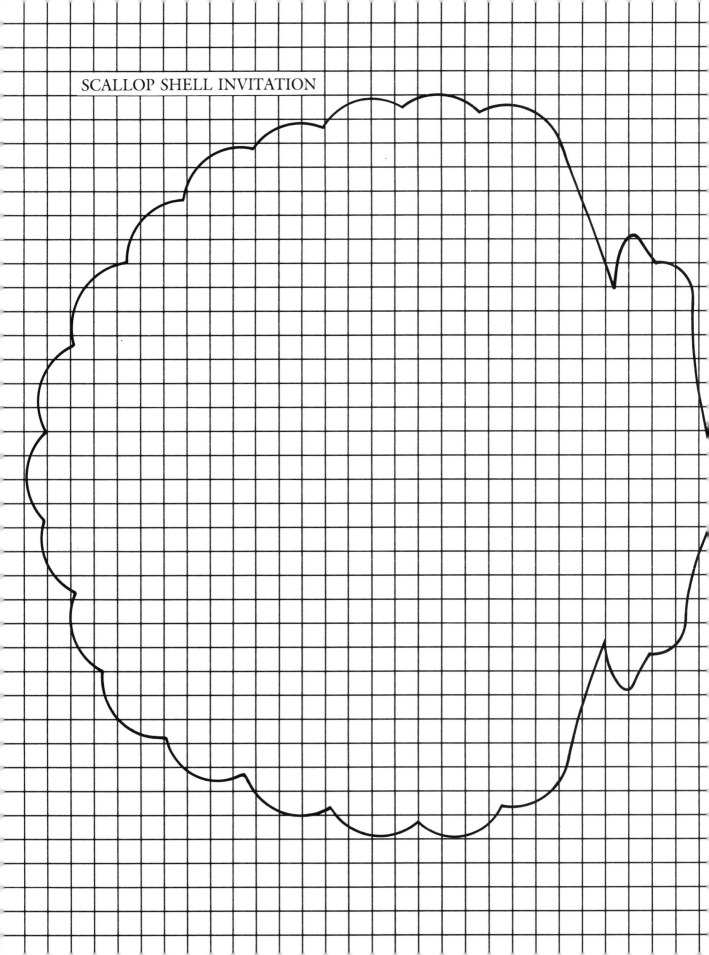

SCALLOP SHELL INVITATION

Cut ribbon into 12″ lengths. Anchor both the ribbon (at its center) and paper shells to the poster board at base of shell, using a stapler. Knot ribbon once around staple and tie a bow (fig. 2). If using a curling ribbon, gently curl ends. Mail in oversize envelopes.

Preparation time: 1¼ hours

SCALLOP SHELL INVITATION

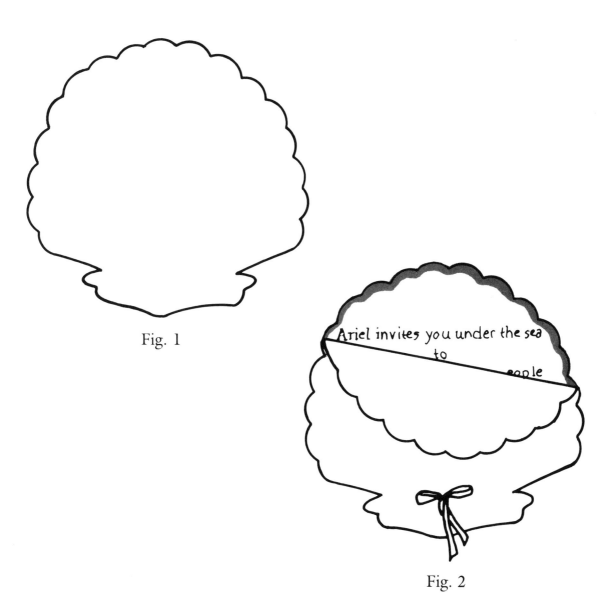

Fig. 1

Ariel invites you under the sea
to
eople

Fig. 2

D E C O R A T I O N S

Any art supply store that carries luau (or Caribbean) paraphernalia is the right place to go for mermaid party supplies. The party room should have seashells, coral branches, and so forth—and, of course, a fishnet over a blue (or green) paper tablecloth. You can also use shells you've collected as vacation souvenirs, or borrow them from friends. For a centerpiece, how about a goldfish bowl with blue gravel and a castle? Add a real goldfish, and you can use it as the grand prize for the Loony Limbo contest. Be sure to have a Chinese food–type take-out carton, lined with a plastic bag, for the winner to take the fish home in.

G E T - A C Q U A I N T E D   A C T I V I T Y

King Triton's Shell Shop

As the guests begin to arrive, gather them together in King Triton's Shell Shop. This can be any room or craft area away from the actual party table. While the children get acquainted with each other, they can also decorate seashells with pastel-colored felt markers.

Surprise! The shells come from the pasta aisle of the supermarket. Buy *jumbo*-size pasta shells for the children to color. These make fun additions to Ariel's Treasure Chest.

F A N T A S Y   F E A T U R E

Ariel's Treasure Chest

Ariel kept many of her precious treasures gathered from sunken ships in a huge treasure chest, hidden away in her secret cave. Among her most prized possessions were a Dinglehopper and a Snarfblat! If you don't have a dozen empty shoeboxes at your house, take up a collection around the neighborhood.

Materials
12 shoe boxes
aluminum foil
brown spray paint
gold cord or ribbon (at least 8 yds.)
scissors
12 gold notary seals
12 sheets gold polyester film
12 plastic bubble pipes
12 small bottles of bubble solution
12 plastic forks
24 tags (strung with ribbon)
12 mesh bags of chocolate coins

THE LITTLE MERMAID PARTY—Flounder's Fruit Salad (p. 87), Under-the-Sea
Biscuits (p. 89), Ursula's Sea Witch Sherbert (p. 92), and Sebastian's Crab Cakes
(p. 94)

Directions

Place boxes and lids, open ends down, on aluminum foil (foil will not stick to the spray-painted materials). Spray boxes and lids, coating thoroughly. Allow to dry for twenty-four hours. Punch two holes, 3″ apart, in the center of each of the short sides of the boxes. Cut 6″ lengths of cord, string them through holes, and knot them on inside of boxes to make handles. Affix a gold notary seal on the center edge of each lid to resemble a latch (fig. 1). Label bubble pipe and fork with tags that say "Snarfblat" and "Dinglehopper" (fig. 2). Line each box with gold polyester film. Arrange a bubble pipe, bottle of bubbles, and a fork in each box, along with a bag of chocolate coins. Place a box at each child's seat. Children can add their decorated pasta shells and game prizes to this favor box.

Note: Gold glitter paint can be used to write one child's name on each box, allowing the boxes to double as place markers.

Preparation time: 1½ hours
Drying time for paint: 24 hours

ARIEL'S TREASURE CHEST

Fig. 1

Fig. 2

Mermaid Marathon

The Mermaid Marathon is basically a relay-style potato-sack race—but the potato sacks are mermaid tails! (See construction information below for making mermaid tails.) The game is played by dividing the children into two teams. The teams line up side by side, with each starting player wearing a mermaid tail like a potato sack. At the signal, players hop across the room (or yard) and around some sort of designated goalpost. When they get back to their team, the next player up puts on the tail and starts hopping. The first team to complete the process wins.

Mermaid Tail Construction Information: Use 4 yards of a *sturdy* green stretch-knit fabric. It should be in tubular knit form. Cut fabric in half, forming two 2-yard lengths. About two-thirds of the way down on each piece, tie a big knot to form a fabric tuft, or "tail" (fig. 1).

Note: Shoes wear out tails fast! Have kids take off their shoes and hop in their stocking feet.

Starfish Fishing

In the Starfish Fishing game, children gather around a plastic wading pool and take turns fishing for plastic starfish. (See construction information below for making plastic starfish.) Tie magnets to the ends of two fishing poles. (You can use yardsticks tied with string instead of fishing poles.) The starfish are weighted down by steel paper clips, which the magnets will attract. The starfish are numbered 1 through 12 to coordinate with assorted grab-bag prizes (wrapped and numbered 1 through 12). If a child should happen to catch two starfish at once, one of the starfish has to be thrown back into the water. When all of the fish have been caught, it's time to pass out the prizes.

Plastic Starfish Construction Information: Cut starfish from colored transparent acetate report covers (about 3" across). Punch one hole in a point on each starfish with a paper punch. Clip jumbo paper clips through the holes. Number the starfish 1 through 12, using a waterproof laundry marker (fig. 2).

Note: Paper clips rust, so don't throw fish in the water-filled wading pool until just before the party starts.

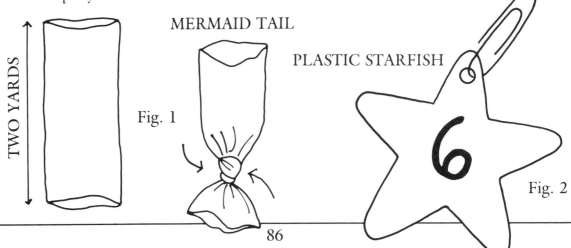

TWO YARDS

MERMAID TAIL

Fig. 1

PLASTIC STARFISH

6

Fig. 2

Loony Limbo

The game begins with two players holding each end of a 6' to 8' bamboo pole at shoulder height. Any other long pole, such as a fishing pole, can also be used. The rest of the players take turns walking under the pole limbo style (leaning backward). After every player has passed under the pole the pole is lowered about 2". This game is easy at first, but it becomes more and more difficult each time the pole is lowered. If a player loses his or her balance, he or she is out.

Note: The first two players out take the ends of the pole so the pole holders can play, too. The final player left—the one who can limbo the lowest—wins.

Remember that goldfish in the table centerpiece? That's the grand prize.

This Caribbean game was made to go with calypso music. The lively beat of "Under the Sea," "Kiss the Girl," and other songs from *The Little Mermaid* are perfect limbo tunes. Encourage the children to sing along, and for extra fun, have a makeshift calypso band accompany the music. Use empty oatmeal boxes for bongos, a toy xylophone for a marimba, and pots, pans, or tin cans to simulate the sound of calypso steel drums.

Menu

FLOUNDER'S FRUIT SALAD

12 servings

Who isn't enchanted by Ariel's adorable little friend, Flounder? Did you ever notice how much Flounder resembles a pear? Well, at this party, Flounder poses as a pear in a fresh fruit salad.

Ingredients
7 medium fresh or canned pears (if fresh, pears should be fairly ripe with no soft brown spots)
¼ cup fruit preservative (to prevent browning of fresh fruit)
8-oz. tub soft cream cheese
blue food coloring
12 miniature marshmallows
12 raisins
12 lettuce leaves (Boston or red leaf)
fresh dill (for garnish)

Directions
Core pears and peel with a vegetable peeler. Cut six pears in half, lengthwise. Slice remaining pear into twelve lengthwise slices. To prevent browning, combine fruit preservative with 3 cups water in a large bowl. Submerge pear halves and slices in this mixture, to coat.

Note: These pears will stay fresh for twelve hours.

One hour before the party, blend cream cheese with food coloring to tint an even shade of deep blue. Fill a small pastry bag, fitted with a #4 round writing tip, and set aside for decorating the salad.

Arrange a lettuce leaf on each plate. Drain the pears and pat dry with paper towels. Place each pear half, cut side down, on a lettuce leaf. Use pear slices to make tails and dorsal fins as shown (fig. 1). Cut a wedge out of the wide end of each pear for Flounder's mouth. Use the wedge to make a lower fin (fig. 2). Pipe cream cheese onto each pear in stripes to resemble Flounder, and press a marshmallow and a raisin into each pear to make an eye (fig. 3). Garnish with dill.

Preparation time: 35 minutes

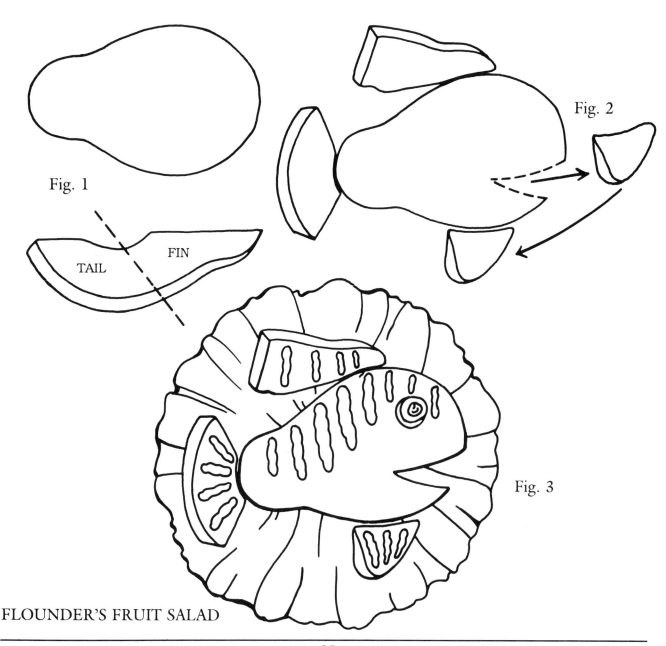

Fig. 1

Fig. 2

TAIL   FIN

Fig. 3

FLOUNDER'S FRUIT SALAD

UNDER-THE-SEA BISCUITS

12 servings

Tuna salad on biscuits shaped like scallop shells makes for thematic—and pretty!—bite-size sandwiches. (For those landlubbers at the party, fill a few biscuits with pimento cheese spread.)

Ingredients
2 cans (10 count) or 3 cans (8 count) extralarge refrigerated biscuits
1 egg, beaten with 1 tbs. water
King Triton's Tuna Salad (recipe follows)
2 3½-oz. jars pimento cheese spread

Directions
Open biscuit cans and separate biscuits. Stretch, slightly, into ovals. For each shell, make deep cut marks at sides of base (fig. 1). Fan out dough to resemble a scallop shell (fig. 2). Cut six slashes halfway through the fan (fig. 3). Place biscuits 3″ apart on an ungreased baking sheet. Lightly brush with beaten egg and bake in a preheated oven for twelve minutes or until golden brown. Cool. Split open and, just before serving, fill with tuna salad (or cheese spread).

Note: Biscuits are best when prepared and baked the morning of the party. However, tuna salad can be made the night before.

UNDER-THE-SEA BISCUITS

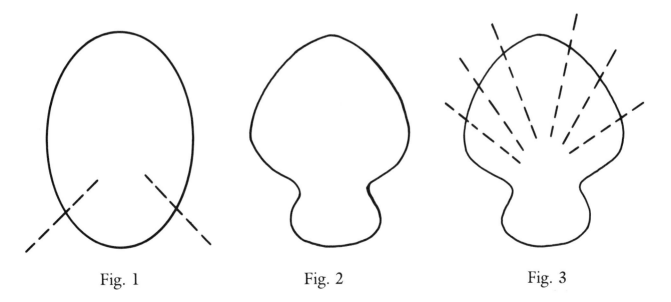

Fig. 1   Fig. 2   Fig. 3

King Triton's Tuna Salad

Ingredients
4 6½-oz. cans solid white tuna (water-packed), drained
⅓ cup chopped celery
⅓ cup chopped scallions
1 tbs. sweet pickle relish
¾ tsp. celery salt
½ tsp. onion powder
⅔ to ¾ cup regular or nonfat mayonnaise
12 lettuce leaves

Directions
Combine tuna, celery, and scallions in a large mixing bowl. Stir relish, celery salt, and onion powder into mayonnaise. Add dressing to tuna and gently toss to combine. Chill until serving time. Serve in seashell biscuits on lettuce.

Preparation time: 20 minutes
Chilling time: 3 hours or overnight

S E A W E E D   S L A W

12 servings

This side dish is a cross between coleslaw and bean salad. French-cut green beans (resembling some sort of undersea fern) are used instead of cabbage.

Ingredients
3 10-oz. pkgs. frozen French-cut green beans
¾ cup regular or nonfat mayonnaise
1 tbs. lemon juice
1 tbs. sugar
½ tsp. dry mustard
½ tsp. salt
1 tsp. onion powder

Directions
Cook beans according to package directions until just tender. Drain thoroughly and chill at least two hours. Meanwhile, combine mayonnaise, lemon juice, sugar, dry mustard, salt, and onion powder until smooth. Toss dressing with beans and chill several hours or overnight.

Preparation time: 12 minutes
Chilling time: 6 hours or overnight

G U P P Y   C U P S

Poor Flounder! Whenever he was frightened, Ariel and the others would call him a "guppy." Guppy Cups are decorated cupcake liners filled with flavored, fish-shaped snack crackers.

Ingredients

1 envelope ranch-style salad-dressing mix
1 tsp. dried dill
¼ cup melted butter or margarine
1 tbs. olive oil
3 cups cheddar-flavored fish-shaped crackers
3 cups pretzel-flavored fish-shaped crackers
12 cupcake liners (try to use white or pale pastel colors)
colored felt-tip marking pens

Directions

Combine salad-dressing mix, dill, butter, and oil in measuring cup and pour into the bottom of a 12″ × 18″ roasting pan. Scatter crackers over seasoning mixture in pan. Gently stir crackers until evenly coated. Preheat oven to 250°F and bake crackers for thirty-five to forty minutes, stirring every ten minutes. Be sure to store in airtight containers to ensure crispness. Crackers may be made up to one week in advance. Use felt-tip markers to draw fish, sea horses, seaweed, etcetera, on cupcake liners. Place crackers in a glass fishbowl, and let kids fill their own Guppy Cups.

Preparation time: 12 minutes
Baking time: 35 to 40 minutes

URSULA'S SEA WITCH SHERBERT

12 servings

Eight licorice legs make each of these frosty little desserts look like an octopus wearing a white whipped-cream wig. You can always substitute the raspberry sherbert with your child's favorite flavor of ice cream, but remember . . . Ursula *is* purple.

Ingredients
black shoelace licorice (about 8 yds.)
6 red gumdrops
24 miniature chocolate chips
1½ cups frozen whipped topping, thawed
½ gal. raspberry sherbert or berry-flavored ice cream or frozen yogurt

Directions
Assemble and freeze the sea witches on a baking sheet or tray covered with aluminum foil. The foil will make the desserts easier to remove from the tray. Just be sure that the tray will fit into your freezer!

Cut the licorice into 3″ lengths and set aside. Slice red gumdrops in half and pinch with your fingers to form twelve sets of lips. Working quickly to prevent melting, use a large ice-cream scoop to place twelve large balls of sherbert on the foil. These scoops are the witches' bodies. Use a small ice-cream scoop to press a smaller ball of sherbert on top of each large one, to form the head. Insert eight licorice legs at the base of each large scoop, twisting at various angles to resemble octopus tentacles (fig. 1). Return the sherbert to the freezer for a few minutes, and fill a small pastry bag, fitted with a #10 round tip, with ½ cup of whipped topping. Fill a second pastry bag, fitted with a large #5 or #7 star tip, with the remaining whipped cream. Remove the sherbert from the freezer and press gumdrop lips into each head. Pipe the whites of eyes onto each face using the round tip, and press chocolate chips into the whipped cream (for pupils). Pipe whipped topping onto each Ursula for hair, standing on end (fig. 2). Keep sea witches in freezer until serving time. Gently lift off foil and onto plates.

Preparation time: 30 minutes
Freezing time: 2 hours or longer

URSULA'S SEA WITCH SHERBERT

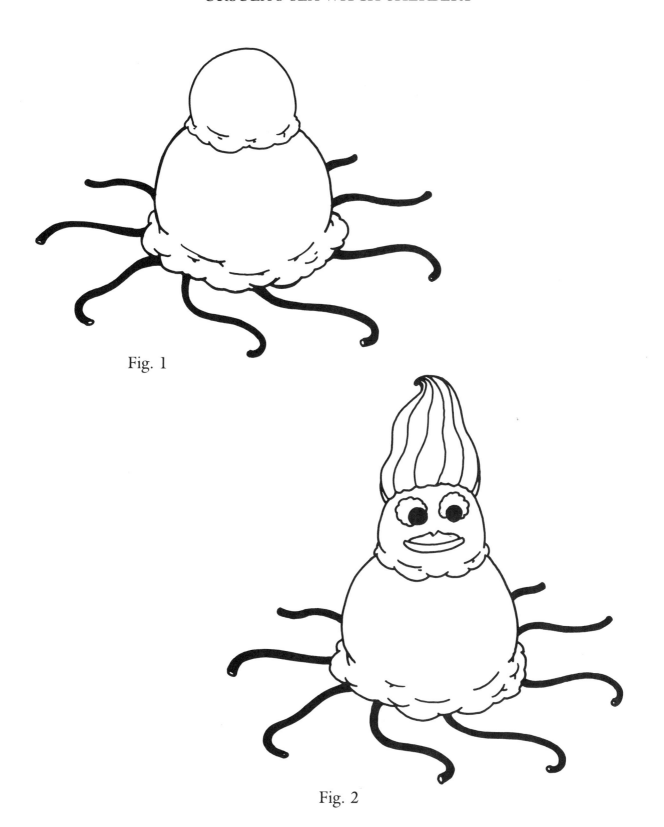

Fig. 1

Fig. 2

SEBASTIAN'S CRAB CAKES

12 servings

Sebastian—the singing, smiling calypso crab—lives in fear of Prince Eric's chef. He is afraid of becoming crab cakes! Don't worry, Sebastian, you're safe. This recipe proves that you can have your crab and eat cake, too.

Ingredients

1⅔ cups flour
1 cup light brown sugar, firmly packed
¼ cup cocoa
1 tsp. baking soda
1½ tsp. salt
1 cup water
⅓ cup vegetable oil
1 tsp. vinegar
½ tsp. vanilla extract
Vanilla Butter Frosting (recipe follows)
blue and red gel food coloring
24 miniature marshmallows
1 tbs. cocoa powder

Directions

Combine flour, brown sugar, cocoa, baking soda, and salt in a mixing bowl and stir. Combine water, oil, vinegar, and vanilla in a measuring cup, and pour over dry ingredients. Mix by hand until completely blended. Pour the mixture into twelve paper-lined medium-size muffin cups. Preheat oven to 350°F and bake cakes for about twenty minutes or until a toothpick inserted in the center comes out clean. Cool completely. Spread a thin layer of vanilla frosting over each cake. Put a stripe of blue gel coloring on the back of a metal spatula. Swirl or color glaze streaks of blue over the surface of the white frosted cupcakes. (This is to suggest water.) Tint the remaining white frosting red. Fill a medium-size pastry bag with frosting. With no end on the nozzle, pipe about a 1″ mound in the center of each cake (fig. 1). Attach a #4 tip and pipe four legs on each side of the mound (fig. 2). Press marshmallows into the top of the mound for eyes. Change to a #10 tip and pipe claws and eyelids (fig. 3). To finish the eyes, press all of the red frosting out of the bag and into a bowl. Blend in enough cocoa powder to tint a deep brown. Spoon frosting back into bag and attach a #4 tip. Squeeze bag just until brown powder begins to come through, pipe pupils on the marshmallow eyes, and pipe a mouth across what is now a face (fig. 4).

  Note: The cakes may be prepared two days in advance.

Vanilla Butter Frosting

Ingredients
1-lb. box confectioners' sugar (sift, if lumpy)
½ cup butter or margarine, softened
1½ tsp. vanilla extract
3 to 4 tbs. milk

Directions
Beat together all ingredients except the milk, which you should add by tablespoons only until the frosting is smooth and of spreading consistency.

Cake preparation time: 20 minutes
Baking time: 20 minutes
Frosting preparation and decoration time: 1 hour

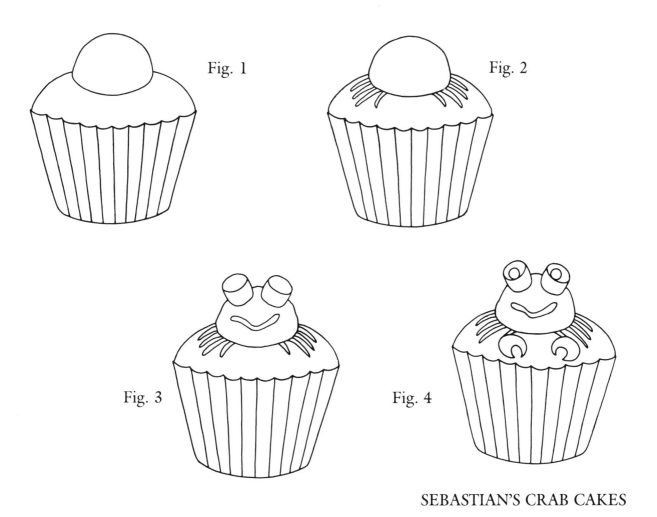

Fig. 1

Fig. 2

Fig. 3

Fig. 4

SEBASTIAN'S CRAB CAKES

C A R I B B E A N B L U E C O O L E R

12 servings

The stranger something seems, the more kids seem to like it. Take, for example, blue soft drinks. Add ginger ale and frozen floating sharks, and you have a Caribbean Blue Cooler.

Ingredients
1 box bite-size shark fruit candies
water
1 pkg. blue soft drink mix
1 2-liter bottle ginger ale

Directions
Prepare shark ice by filling four ice cube trays two-thirds full with water. Allow them to stand at room temperature for one hour to remove air bubbles. (Cloudy ice occurs when you fill trays from a running faucet, and you want this ice to be as clear as possible.) Place two sharks of the *same* color in each cube section. The sharks will dissolve slightly, tinting ice cubes lovely pastel shades. Don't combine two different colors of sharks or you'll have "muddy" colored ice. Freeze the trays for at least four hours until firm. Prepare soft drink mix per package directions. To serve drinks, drop about two or three different colors of ice in each clear plastic drinking cup. Fill cups halfway with blue soft drink. Fill the rest of the cups with ginger ale. Have the beverages chilled so that the ice will melt slowly. The sharks will no longer be solid candies by the time the ice dissolves. They take on a soft marshmallowlike texture.

Preparation time: 15 minutes
Freezing time: 4 hours

Ages 6 to 12

*C*inderella is the dramatic story of a girl of noble birth who is mistreated by her cruel stepmother and stepsisters. On the night of the royal ball, Cinderella's Fairy Godmother transforms her out of her rags and into a vision of beauty just in time to meet Prince Charming. At the stroke of midnight, when Cinderella has to run off and leave the prince, she accidentally leaves behind a glass slipper. The king orders the grand duke to search for the slipper's owner, and when he matches it to Cinderella's foot, Cinderella and the prince are reunited forever.

Invitation: See-through Slipper

Decorations: Castle Motif—balloon chandelier; wrapping-paper red carpet; paper lace tablecloth; "fine china" paper plates; Golden Tiaras

Get-acquainted Activity: Candy Crown Jewels

Fantasy Feature: Golden Tiaras

Games: Dress-up Dash; The Cinder Sweep; Cinderella's Designer Gown

Menu: Crudités Coach; Princess Pasta; Bread-stick Brooms; Frosty Ice-cream Pumpkins; Cinderella's Castle Cake; Glass Slipper Soda

See-through Slipper

A slip of a shoe you can see right through, and it slides right into an envelope! The invitation is made out of a transparent piece of plastic acetate.

Materials
12 8½″ × 11″ sheets clear plastic acetate, or 6 clear report covers, split in half along fold
tracing paper
1 sheet thin poster board
pencil
rubber cement
1 tube gold glitter paint (squeezable)
black felt-tip laundry marker
12 9″ × 12″ white envelopes
12 gold notary seals
gold ink pen
scissors

Directions
With tracing paper and pencil, trace the shoe pattern on page 99. Cut the tracing out, and glue it to the poster board. Cut the poster board shoe out to make a stencil, and then cut a large slipper shape out of each piece of acetate. Outline the edges of each slipper with glitter paint, and write the following message on each one:

Princess (guest's name)'s

   presence is requested

      at the grand ballroom

         of (your child's name)'s palace

           for a royal birthday party

           (your address)

              on (date) at (time)

                RSVP on royal phone line

              (your phone number)

Slip invitations into envelopes, and close with notary seal for an official look. Address envelopes with gold ink pen.

Preparation time: 1¼ hours

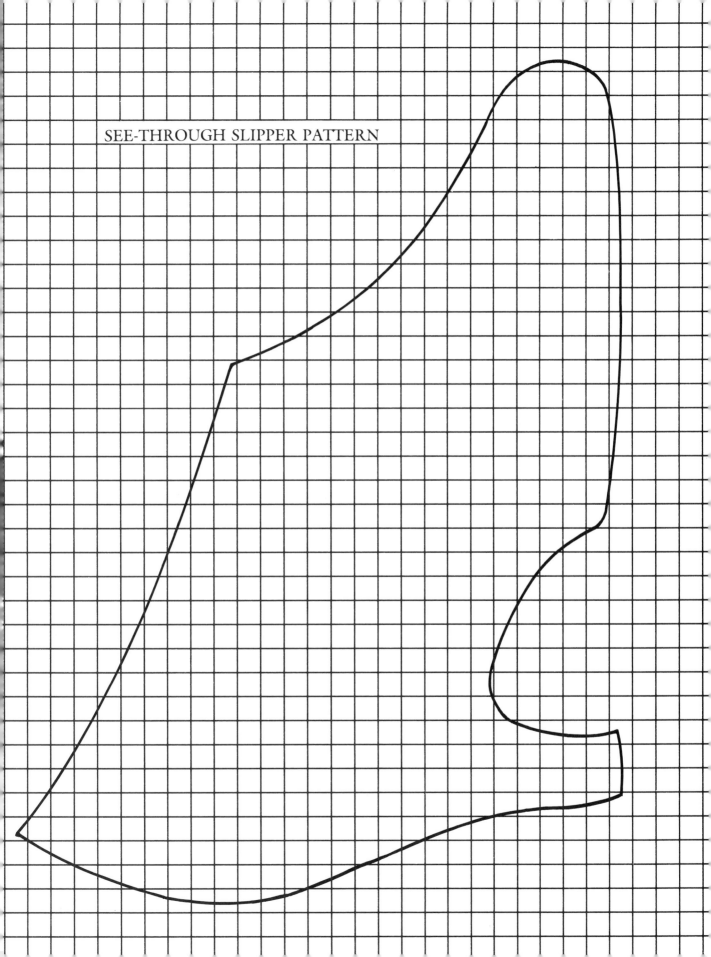

SEE-THROUGH SLIPPER PATTERN

D E C O R A T I O N S

Your home is your castle . . . but for this party, it becomes the Crown Prince's palace. For an opulent touch, try making a tiered chandelier from balloons. Use oblong white or silvery balloons, and hang them in a bouquet from the ceiling. Add strips of rainbow cellophane and streamers of rainbow ribbon for the shimmering effect of crystal. Appoint a royal officer at the door to announce the entrance of each visiting princess—fanfare from a kazoo trumpet gives it an official touch. You can even roll out the red carpet with a roll of red wrapping paper. Set the table with a paper lace tablecloth. Decorate paper plates with gold felt-tip markers around the rims, imitating fine china. Display fantasy-feature tiaras on each plate. Cinderella's Castle Cake takes its place of prominence as the centerpiece. At one end of the table, set the Crudités Coach. At the other end, serve Glass Slipper Soda from a punch bowl.

G E T - A C Q U A I N T E D   A C T I V I T Y

Candy Crown Jewels

For the opening activity, spearmint sapphires, raspberry rubies, and edible emeralds are laced on licorice necklaces. After each princess makes her entrance to your child's party, escort her to the crown jeweler. This is a table set up with bowls of every kind of candy with holes (hard candies, fruit gels, etc.) and even donut-shaped cereal. Guests thread their own necklaces or bracelets on long strings of red licorice and then knot the ends together.

F A N T A S Y   F E A T U R E

Golden Tiaras

Look for gold foil at your local florist or art supply store.

Materials
12 ½"- to ¾"-wide plastic headbands
6 yds. 30"-wide gold florist foil
hobby glue
scissors
large colored sequins

CINDERELLA PARTY—Cinderella's Castle Cake (p. 108)

Directions

Cut the foil into ½-yard lengths so that you have 12 18″ × 30″ pieces. For each tiara, fold the foil in half, into an 18″ × 15″ rectangle (fig. 1). Fold it in half again, into a 9″ × 15″ rectangle (fig. 2), and mold it around the contours of the headband (fig. 3). There should be about 8″ of foil extending from the headband. Pinch the foil at intervals to create a scalloped effect. Twist excess foil back at the ends, and glue sequins across the headband (fig. 4).

Preparation time: 1 hour

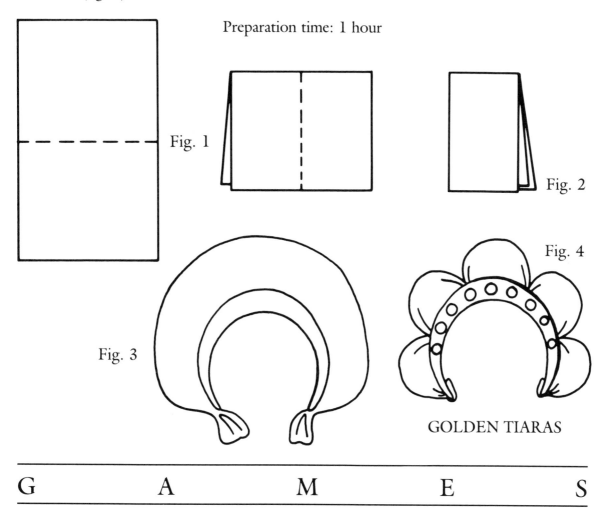

Fig. 1

Fig. 2

Fig. 3

Fig. 4

GOLDEN TIARAS

G   A   M   E   S

Dress-up Dash

On the night of the royal ball, Cinderella was always in a hurry. First she had to rush to reach the palace, and then she had to run home early—leaving her legendary slipper behind.

For this dress-up race, you'll need two suitcases with similar apparel: an oversize dress or jacket (for the girls to pull on over their clothing), a hat, some jewelry, and facsimiles of a glass slipper. (You can use a pair of clear plastic beach sandals and put one sandal in each suitcase.) Players are divided into two teams and line up across the room from the suitcases. The first player on each team is given a magic wand (see Sleeping

Beauty Party, Fantasy Feature, page 153). At the sound of twelve chimes (or bongs on a pan), the race begins. Two players rush to the suitcases, each one taps it with her wand, opens it, and puts on everything in the suitcase. The players then take everything back off, put the clothing back in the suitcase, close it, pick up the wand, and rush back to tag the next player on their team. (Each player must first be tapped on the head by the wand before taking it for the next round.) The first team to finish wins the title Best Dressed.

The Cinder Sweep

In the Cinder Sweep, colored confetti cinders are swept into the opposing team's territory to score a goal. You'll need about eight cups of colored confetti, twelve brooms—you may want to ask guests to bring their own, when they RSVP—and two folding fireplace or makeshift screens.

Set up the game in a large unfurnished area with a smooth floor (no carpeting). Stand a screen at each end of the room, and pour confetti in a line across the center of the room. Divide the players into two teams. Each team appoints offensive and defensive players. Offensive players line up at the center line, and defensive players guard their screen. At a signal, the match begins. The offensive players try to sweep as much confetti as they can into the opposing team's screen while the defense struggles to sweep incoming confetti out. After five or six minutes, the closing signal sounds and the game comes to an end. The winning team is the one with the most confetti in the other team's area. (If it's a close call, sweep up each team's confetti in a dust pan, and pour it into a glass measuring cup for a final judgment.)

Cinderella's Designer Gown

When Cinderella first received word of the ball, she didn't have a thing to wear. She found an old pink dress left by her mother, but it was much too plain for such a grand party. Alas! She left it up in the attic and went about her dreary chores. But her little friends, the birds and mice, were quite resourceful. They gathered beads, ribbon, lace, and a lovely sash—cast off by Cinderella's stepsisters. With a bit of tailoring, they designed a new dress for Cinderella to wear. (Of course, the stepsisters later recognized their trimmings on Cinderella and ripped up the dress. It was up to Cinderella's Fairy Godmother to whip up a new one.)

In this activity, children pretend that they are the birds and mice. It's up to them to transform an otherwise frumpy frock with odds and ends. Draw a basic gown on a large chalkboard with an easel stand. Provide a box of colored chalk. Children take turns adding one distinctive feature to the dress. Design by committee frequently results in outrageous fashion . . . but that's what makes it fun. Since this isn't a game, there are no winners or losers. It's over when the dress is done, but don't be surprised if the children want to erase it and start another one!

Menu

C R U D I T É S   C O A C H

12 servings

Here's Cinderella's classic carriage, created from a pumpkin . . . well, so to speak. Pumpkins aren't available year-round, but you can achieve the same effect with a large butternut squash. Children will enjoy eating veggies dipped into the golden coach, which is pulled by white-radish horses.

Ingredients
1 large butternut squash
lemon juice
2 doz. white radishes (3″ to 4″ long)
8 cloves
6 almond slivers
4 scallions
2 doz. regular toothpicks (see note, page x)
4 frilled party toothpicks (see note, page x)
Imperial Golden Onion Dip (recipe follows)
Vegetable Dippers (instructions follow)

Directions
Cut the neck off the butternut squash, just above the base, and slice four ¾″ slices from the neck for carriage wheels (fig. 1). Hollow out the base of the squash, leaving about a ¾″-thick shell on all sides. Brush the inside of the squash and all exposed sides of the slices with lemon juice to prevent browning. Anchor the wheels in place with regular toothpicks (fig. 2). For each horse, use toothpicks to attach four radish legs to a radish body (fig. 3). Cut another radish 1″ from the tip at an angle (fig. 4). Reposition with a frilly toothpick to form head and neck. Stick in clove eyes and almond ears (fig. 5). Attach the neck to the body. Make a scallion tail by trimming the stems from the root of a scallion (fig. 6). Soak the stems in ice water to make the ends fan out. Attach one tail to each body (fig. 7).

    Note: This project should be prepared the day before the party, no sooner or later. Keep the coach, the horses, and the vegetables for dipping wrapped in plastic and chilled in the refrigerator. Store the dip separately. Assemble the carriage before serving by arranging the horses in front of the coach in the center of a large oval platter. Surround the platter with vegetables, and fill the coach with dip.

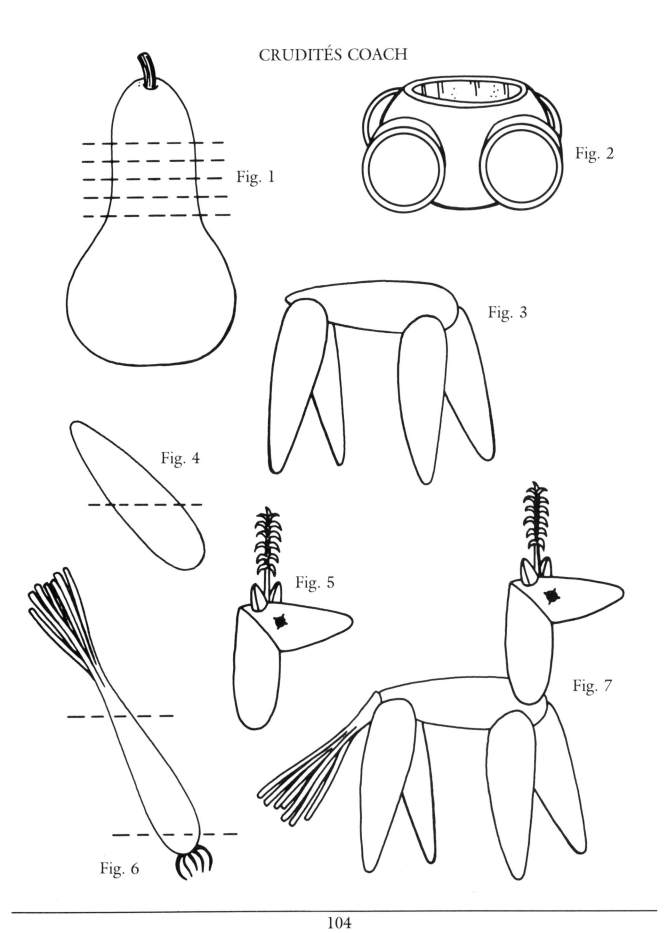

CRUDITÉS COACH

Fig. 1

Fig. 2

Fig. 3

Fig. 4

Fig. 5

Fig. 6

Fig. 7

Imperial Golden Onion Dip

Ingredients
1 tbs. lemon juice
2 tsp. curry powder
2 tbs. sugar
2 tbs. dry onion soup mix
⅔ cup regular or nonfat mayonnaise
1 cup sour cream or low-fat yogurt

Directions
Blend the ingredients together and chill overnight to develop flavors.

Vegetable Dippers

Ingredients
1 bunch broccoli
1 bunch cauliflower
1 bunch celery
1 bunch carrots

Directions
Break broccoli and cauliflower into flowerets. Blanch in boiling water for ten seconds. Plunge into ice water and drain. Trim celery, and cut into sticks. Scrape carrots, and cut into sticks. Store in plastic bags in the refrigerator.

Total preparation time: 1½ hours
Chilling time: 24 hours

P R I N C E S S P A S T A

12 servings

Three colors of pasta make an otherwise ordinary dish into a meal fit for a princess. Curly rotini, mostaccioli, and even old-fashioned macaroni can be found in flavor-blend boxes (regular, tomato, and spinach pasta all together). For an extra treat, try using cheese-filled tricolor tortellini.

Ingredients

1 16-oz. box tricolor pasta (rotini, mostaccioli, macaroni,
or cheese-filled tortellini)
2 lbs. lean ground beef or turkey
1 lb. sliced mushrooms
1 tbs. olive oil (use only if beef is *very lean,* or with turkey)
3 16-oz. jars marinara sauce
1 15-oz. can stewed tomatoes
½ cup sliced ripe olives
½ cup grated Parmesan cheese

Directions

Cook pasta according to package directions. Drain. Meanwhile, sauté meat and mushrooms in an extralarge skillet (using olive oil if meat is very lean). When meat is thoroughly browned and mushrooms are cooked, stir in marinara sauce, tomatoes, and olives. Cover and simmer over low heat for eight to ten minutes. Toss pasta together with sauce and cheese. Serve at once.

Note: This dish can be prepared a day or two in advance, then reheated when ready to serve.

Preparation time: 25 to 30 minutes

B R E A D - S T I C K   B R O O M S

2 dozen

Cinderella was so named because one of her tasks was to sweep up chimney soot, or cinders. These bread-stick brooms are perfectly paired with Princess Pasta.

Ingredients
3 cans (8 count) refrigerated bread sticks
1 egg, slightly beaten
poppy seeds

Directions
Separate the bread sticks and unroll them, stretching to about 10″ or 12″. Tie a knot in each stick, about 3″ from one end. Cut four slits in each short end to resemble a tassel (fig. 1). Arrange the bread sticks about 3″ apart on baking sheets coated with a nonstick cooking spray. Spread the tassels slightly. Brush the bread sticks with beaten egg and sprinkle the handles with poppy seeds (fig. 2). Bake in a 350°F oven for fifteen to eighteen minutes. Serve at once.

Note: These may be prepared a day in advance. Reheat in 200°F oven for eight minutes.

Preparation time: 15 minutes
Baking time: 15 to 18 minutes

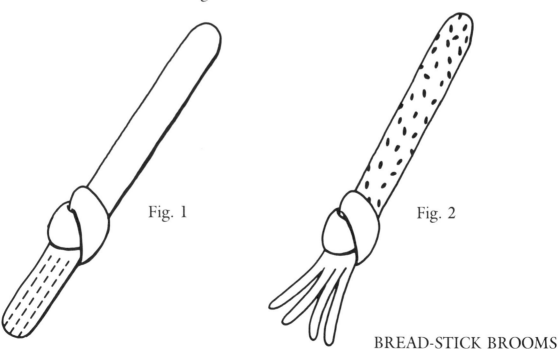

Fig. 1

Fig. 2

BREAD-STICK BROOMS

FROSTY ICE-CREAM PUMPKINS

12 servings

Ingredients
1 qt. pumpkin ice cream or orange sherbert
12 cinnamon sticks

Directions
Place twelve large scoops of ice cream or sherbert on a cookie sheet lined with aluminum foil (fig. 1). Use the rounded-edge handle of a wooden spoon to score section each scoop to resemble a pumpkin, and insert a cinnamon stick for the stem (fig. 2). Freeze pumpkins at least eight hours before serving.

   Note: Pumpkins may be prepared up to three days in advance, covered with plastic wrap, and frozen.

Preparation time: 5 to 10 minutes
Freezing time: 8 hours or overnight

Fig. 1

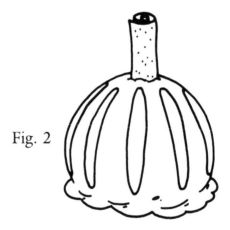

Fig. 2

FROSTY ICE-CREAM PUMPKINS

CINDERELLA'S CASTLE CAKE

12+ servings

With its tall towers and distinctive arch, Disney's version of Cinderella's castle is instantly recognizable the world over. You can create a dramatic castle cake with the help of a basic ring mold.

Ingredients

3⅓ cups flour
2½ cups sugar
1 cup shortening
1¾ cups milk
4¾ tsp. baking powder
1 tsp. salt
2 tsp. almond extract
8 egg whites
½ cup multicolored confetti-candy bits
Blue Buttercream Frosting (recipe follows)
Chocolate Towers (instructions follow)
2 1.55-oz. milk chocolate bars
48 to 50 milk chocolate candies
Tinted Coconut (instructions follow)

Directions

Combine the flour, sugar, shortening, milk, baking powder, salt, and almond extract in a large mixing bowl. Beat with an electric mixer on medium speed for thirty seconds. Beat on high speed for two minutes. Add the egg whites, and beat for an additional two minutes on high speed. Fold in the confetti candy. Line two 8″-square pans with baking parchment. Grease and flour a 10″ 6-cup ring mold. Fill the ring mold two-thirds full. Divide the remaining batter between the square pans. Preheat the oven to 350°F, and bake the cakes for thirty-five to forty minutes or until a toothpick inserted in the center of the cakes comes out clean. Cool the cakes completely, and invert from pans.

Note: This cake is really too large to freeze in its finished state. To prepare in advance, cakes may be frozen at this stage.

Cover a 12″ × 24″ board with aluminum foil. Prepare the frosting and the towers. Level the rounded surface of the ring cake and the square cakes with a knife. Cut the ring cake into two semicircles, and sandwich the sections together (back to back) with frosting. Stack the square cakes together with a layer of frosting in between. Cut through the layers, down the middle, to make two 8″ × 4″ rectangles. Place the arch, cut side down, in the center of the board. Stand a rectangular cake along each side of the arch (fig. 1). Cover all the surfaces with frosting, even underneath the arch (fig. 2). Place two double-tiered Chocolate Towers on each of the side cakes. Invert the remaining two flat-bottomed chocolate cones in the center of the arch, side by side (fig. 3). Cut each chocolate bar into twelve segments, and use them for doors and windows on the front and back of the cake. Line the edges of the castle with candies for battlements (fig. 4). Surround the castle with green coconut grass.

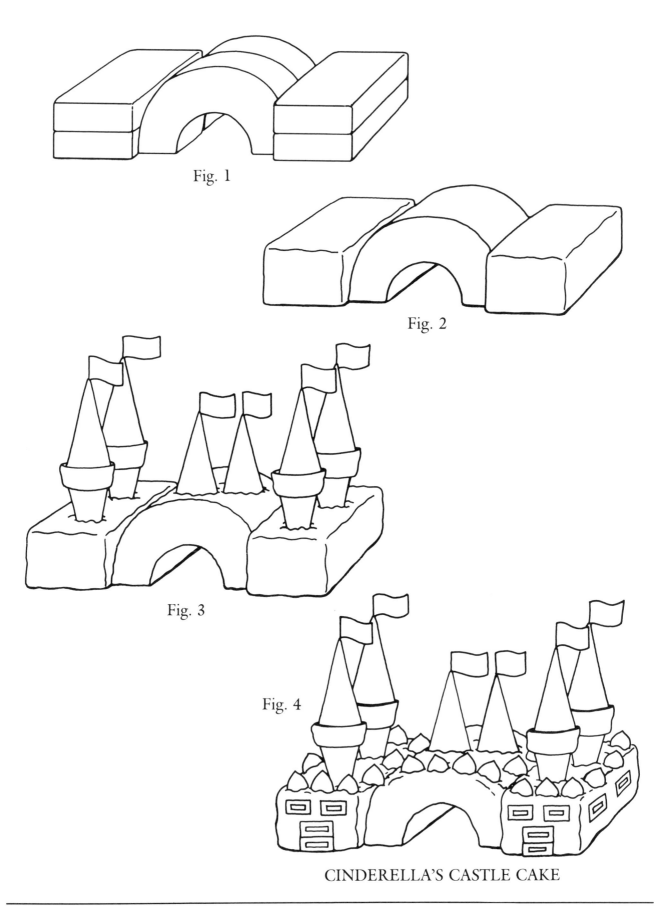

Fig. 1

Fig. 2

Fig. 3

Fig. 4

CINDERELLA'S CASTLE CAKE

Blue Buttercream Frosting

Ingredients
1½ cups butter or margarine, softened
1 tbs. vanilla extract
10 cups confectioners' sugar
6 to 8 tbs. milk
blue gel food coloring

Directions
Cream butter and vanilla until light and fluffy. Beat in sugar and enough milk to make frosting smooth and spreadable. Tint the frosting a delicate shade of pale blue.

Chocolate Towers

Ingredients
8 oz. milk chocolate chips or chopped chocolate
2 tbs. vegetable shortening
4 flat-bottomed ice-cream cones
6 sugar cones (pointed)
6 colored paper flags on toothpicks (see note, page x)

Directions
Melt the chocolate and the shortening in the top of a double boiler (or two minutes in the microwave), stirring until smooth. Hold each cone over the pan, and then cover evenly with chocolate, allowing excess to drip off. Invert the cones on foil, and chill to set the chocolate. Turn the flat-bottomed cones right side up. Push flags into the pointed ends of the sugar cones. Fit the sugar cones, open ends down, on top of the open ends of the four flat-bottomed cones. The remaining two sugar cones will be inverted on the center of the cake.

Tinted Coconut

Ingredients
2 to 3 cups shredded coconut
1 tbs. water
green gel food coloring

Directions

Place a drop or two of green gel food coloring in 1 tbs. of water. Add the water to a one-quart jar filled with 2 to 3 cups of coconut. Shake vigorously until the coconut is evenly tinted.

Total preparation time: 1½ hours
Baking time: 35 to 40 minutes

G L A S S   S L I P P E R   S O D A

12 + servings

Ice molds are an easy alternative to ice carvings. These fancy sculptures are frequently featured on buffets. Flexible rubber molds are filled with water and frozen. When firm, the molds are simply pulled off the ice figures. Guess what? You can create a pair of frosty glass slippers using this same technique and a pair of rubber shoe protectors. (Be sure to use a brand-new, never-worn pair!)

Choose a woman's style with a flat heel. (High-heel styles have holes for the heels—also, the angled position makes them difficult to fill with fluid.) If you can't find a woman's flat shoe, you can resort to a small-size man's shoe.

Ingredients

1 2-liter bottle lemon-lime soda
⅓ cup grenadine syrup

Directions

Thoroughly wash the shoe protectors inside and out. Fill them with water and pour the water into a glass measuring cup (to determine how much the shoes will hold). Pour out the water and fill the measuring cup with the same amount of flat soda. (Allow the soda for shoes to go flat. Cap the rest to preserve carbonation.) Place the shoe protectors in a level pan and fill them with flat soda. Freeze for twenty-four hours. Meanwhile, chill the remaining soda. To serve, pour grenadine into the bottom of a large punch bowl. Fill with about four cups of soda. Carefully peel away the shoe protectors from the ice and place the slippers in bowl. Cover them with the remaining soda and serve immediately.

Note: Ice slippers may be frozen, wrapped in plastic, for up to a week in advance.

Preparation time: 15 minutes
Standing time for soda: 2 to 3 hours
Freezing and chilling time: 24 hours

KING OF THE WILD FRONTIER PARTY

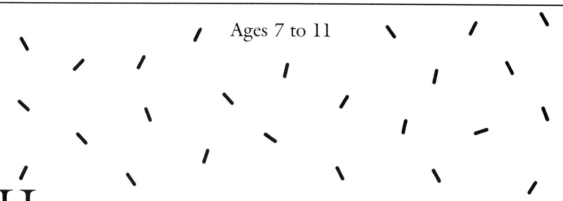

Ages 7 to 11

Hunter, scout, soldier, congressman—the colorful career of Davy Crockett made him one of America's favorite real-life folk heroes of the 1800s. From the Tennessee mountains to Washington, D.C., to the Alamo, Davy Crockett was there. Known for his heroism, hunting skills, tall tales, and down-home charm, Crockett was the hero of a Walt Disney television series in the 1950s.

Invitation: Tennessee Volunteers Poster

Decorations: Wilderness Motif—leaves, branches; pinecones; stuffed animals (bears, skunks, raccoons, etc.)

Get-acquainted Activity: Custom-made Coonskin Caps

Fantasy Feature: Bowie Knife Cookies

Games: Coonskin Grinning Contest; Keelboat Race; "Remember the Alamo!"

Menu: Tennessee Valley Greens; Barbecued Baby Boar; Tomahawk Potatoes; Bear Paw Biscuits (with Honey Butter); Davy Crockett's Cocoa Log Cabin Cake; Ice-cream Raccoons; Georgie's Ginger Mountain Brew

Tennessee Volunteers Poster

An invitation to a frontier party would most appropriately be posted on a tree. However, pretend pioneers have to be practical and spread the word through the mail instead. Still, by the time you finish with these invitations, they'll look like posters that were nailed up in the woods during wartime.

Materials
6 to 12 large brown paper grocery bags
scissors
pencil
sharp-edged ruler
black felt-tip laundry marker
distressing tools: nails, thick screw, damp used teabag, catsup
12 9″ × 12″ brown envelopes

Directions
Cut apart the fronts and backs of grocery bags. (If there is printing on the front, then just use the backs of twelve bags.) With a pencil and ruler, outline an 8½″ × 11″ page on the brown paper. Hold ruler firmly along pencil lines and tear around outline to produce a feathered edge. Punch nail holes at either corner. Similarly, push a thick screw through paper in two places to create a couple of bullet holes. (You can even add a small tear or slash from an arrowhead.) Sprinkle paper with water to give it the weathered effect of rain. Age the paper further by rubbing it in places with the damp used tea bag. Finally, add a few spots of catsup for blood stains. Allow the posters twenty-four hours to dry, preferably in the sun. Once dry, hand print the following message on each one using the black felt-tip laundry marker:

The Tennessee Volunteers
are recruiting scouts.
Please report to the
(your child's name) Campsite
on (date) at (time)
in the territory of (your address)
RSVP: Call (your phone number) and tell 'em Davy Crockett sent you

Mail in 9″ × 12″ envelopes.

Preparation time: 1½ hours
Drying time: 24 hours

D E C O R A T I O N S

If you can't hold the party in your backyard, this wild and woodsy feast calls for bringing the outdoors in. Cover a large table with a green paper tablecloth. Collect leaves, branches, pinecones, and interesting stones to decorate the table. Small stuffed animals such as skunks, raccoons, and teddy bears add to the effect. Use Bowie Knife Cookies as place markers. Davy Crockett's Cocoa Log Cabin Cake acts as a centerpiece, and the Barbecued Baby Boar should be set at the head of the table.

G E T - A C Q U A I N T E D   A C T I V I T Y

Custom-made Coonskin Caps

So simple, and no raccoon need suffer! As the Tennessee Volunteers arrive, let them custom tailor their own tissue-paper coonskin caps for a perfect fit.

Materials
24 20″ × 30″ sheets gray tissue paper
¾″ or 1″ black plastic electrical tape
scissors

Directions
Use doubled sheets of paper for each hat. Gather papers at each of the narrower (20″) ends, and tightly bind them with a little tape (fig. 1). Tuck one end under at the crown, and tape down if necessary (fig. 2). Place on head for fit, and gather at the back. Anchor with tape (fig. 3). Spread the paper slightly to make a puffy tail. Loosely band two or three pieces of tape on tail for stripes (fig. 4).

Preparation time: 10 minutes per hat

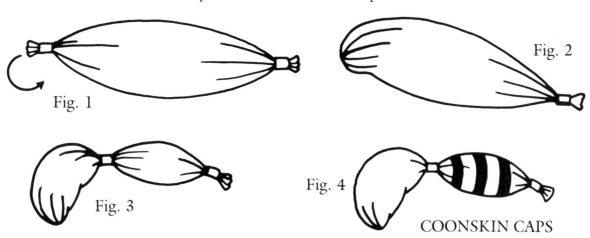

Fig. 1

Fig. 2

Fig. 3

Fig. 4

COONSKIN CAPS

Bowie Knife Cookies

3 dozen

Some parents may have objections to any type of play knife. But a frontier party would seem incomplete without a reference to Davy Crockett's friend Jim Bowie. Bowie designed a new style of hunting knife that revolutionized the American westward movement. But don't worry, Mom: Cookie knives seldom stimulate aggressive play. For those children who don't eat them immediately, any swashbuckling attempts will end in crumbs.

Ingredients
1½ cups confectioners' sugar
1 cup butter or margarine, softened
1 egg
1 tsp. vanilla extract
2½ cups flour
1 tsp. baking soda
1 tsp. cream of tartar
Chocolate Icing (recipe follows)

Directions
Cream sugar and butter together. Blend in egg and vanilla. Combine dry ingredients in a separate bowl, then add to the butter and egg mixture. Blend to make a smooth dough. Wrap dough in plastic wrap and refrigerate for at least two hours. Trace Bowie Knife Cookie pattern on page 118 onto waxed paper. Cut out waxed-paper knife and use for your cookie pattern. Divide dough in half and keep one part chilled while working on the other. Roll dough out on a floured surface (wooden board, marble, or pastry cloth) until it's about ¼" thick. Place pattern on dough and cut around it using an embroidery needle. (A needle works much better than a knife because it can cut in all directions.) Carefully lift cookies with a spatula and place on a cookie sheet lined with baking parchment, about 1" apart from each other. Bake in a preheated 375°F oven for seven to eight minutes or until delicately golden. Cool completely and remove from paper. Scraps may be rerolled after briefly chilling.

Note: Dough or complete cookies may be made a week in advance.

KING OF THE WILD FRONTIER PARTY—Ice-cream Raccoons (p. 128)

Chocolate Icing

Ingredients
2 cups confectioners' sugar
2 tbs. cocoa
5 to 6 tbs. cream

Directions
Blend together until consistency is smooth, adding more or less cream as needed. Then fill a small pastry bag fitted with a #2 round writing tip. Outline handle (fig. 1), and write one child's name on each knife to use as a place marker. Write "Bowie Knife" on the remaining cookies (fig. 2).

Preparation time: 1¼ hours
Chilling time: 2 hours or longer
Baking time: 2 batches, 7 to 8 minutes each

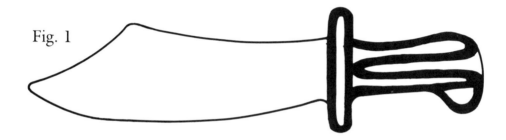

Fig. 1

BOWIE KNIFE COOKIES

Fig. 2

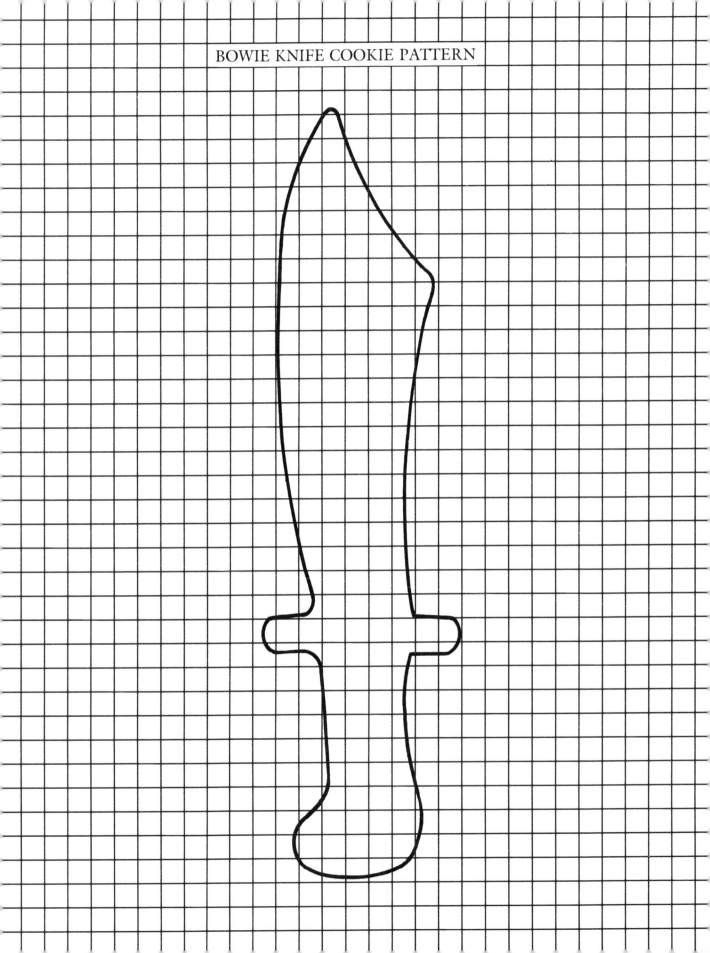

BOWIE KNIFE COOKIE PATTERN

Coonskin Grinning Contest

It was said that Davy Crockett could "grin down any critter in the forest." According to one folk tale, he flashed his friendly smile at a raccoon and it jumped right out of its skin! That's how Davy came to have his legendary coonskin cap.

In this game, Davy Crockett captures all of the critters in the forest by grinning them down. Write the names of eleven forest creatures—raccoon, squirrel, beaver, badger, chipmunk, opossum, deer, turtle, owl, bear, and fox—on self-adhesive tags. On a twelfth tag, write "Davy Crockett." Shuffle all of the tags in a hat, and have each player draw one out. Each child wears his or her tag, and together, the forest animals form a large circle around Davy, who stands in the middle.

Similar to a stare-down contest, Davy makes eye contact with one of the players. Davy flashes a toothy smile at the animal, who must try to maintain a straight face. If the animal giggles or cracks up, Davy takes him or her captive and the player must sit inside the circle, next to Davy. If Davy giggles or breaks his or her smile first, then Davy and the animal switch places (and get new name tags). This game continues until, eventually, all of the critters are captured.

Keelboat Race

Davy Crockett may have been King of the Wild Frontier, but Mike Fink was King of the River. Mike Fink was the best boat captain on the Ohio and Mississippi rivers. When he challenged Davy Crockett and Georgie Russel to a race down to New Orleans, he didn't expect any real competition. The two crews pushed their keelboats along shallow rivers with the aid of long poles. Davy and Georgie surprised everyone by winning the race, despite running into many obstacles, including the rapids!

For this game, you'll need two skateboards, two poles (ski poles, bamboo rods, even canes), and some empty plastic soda-pop bottles. Using the bottles, set up an obstacle course on the "Ohio River" (any flat surface suitable for skateboarding). In poling down the river, players have to weave around the rapids (the soda bottles).

Divide the children into two teams: Mike Fink's crew on the *Gullywumper,* and Davy Crockett's crew on the *Bertha Mae*. Teams line up side by side in Maysville, Kentucky (the beginning of the obstacle course). Explain how a keelboat is poled, or pushed down the river. The object is to sit cross-legged on the keelboat (skateboard) and push it along, using the pole. Players may *not* use their hands or feet! Each team sends a player downstream, in and out of the rapids, to the finish line, and back upstream again. When players return to their team, the next crew member in line boards the keelboat. If a player uses his or her hands or feet, knocks down the rapids, or capsizes the keelboat, he or she is considered a "man overboard." Any man overboard has to go back to Maysville and start over. In this relay race, the first crew to finish is the winning team.

"Remember the Alamo!"

Davy Crockett died in 1836, defending the Alamo in San Antonio, Texas. In this game, however, history has yet to be determined. A Spanish mission is constructed out of large cardboard boxes (fig. 1) and given a paper Alamo flag to display (fig. 2). Now your backyard or recreation room is ready to stage this famous siege.

First divide the children into two teams: the Mexican army of General Santa Anna and the Texas Independence Movement, which included Davy Crockett, Georgie Russel, and Jim Bowie. Next, issue food and ammunition to each army. In this case, they're one and the same: puffed-corn cereal! Teams face off on opposite sides of the Alamo and cannot come within four feet of the walls. One box of cereal is given to each team and the puffed-corn bullets are divided among the players. At the signal, the Mexican army begins the attack, tossing cereal at the Alamo. The Texans may retaliate by hurling their puffed-corn at the Mexicans. Both armies may reuse any ammunition that falls within their territory and volley it back at the enemy. However, any cereal that falls within four feet of the Alamo walls (on either side) cannot be touched. Hungry soldiers who choose to eat their ammunition hurt their cause. The outcome of the battle is determined when one team runs out of puffed-corn. They must wave a white flag in the air and surrender.

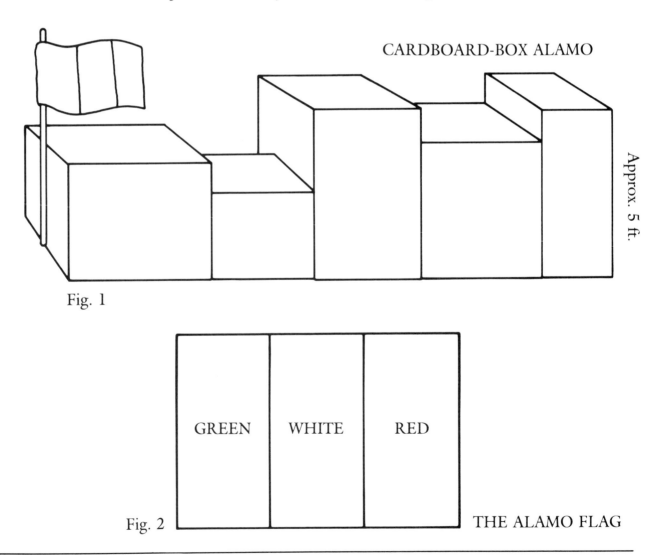

CARDBOARD-BOX ALAMO

Approx. 5 ft.

Fig. 1

GREEN	WHITE	RED

Fig. 2

THE ALAMO FLAG

Menu

TENNESSEE VALLEY GREENS

12 servings

Most children like ranch-style salad dressings. This homemade buttermilk version features fresh dill.

Ingredients
8 cups shredded red leaf lettuce
8 cups shredded fresh spinach
¾ cup regular or nonfat mayonnaise
⅔ cup buttermilk
½ tsp. celery salt
½ tsp. onion powder
¼ tsp. cracked pepper
2 tbs. fresh dill, chopped (or 2 tsp. dried)

Directions
Wash lettuce and spinach. Dry and chill in the refrigerator until serving time. Meanwhile, combine the remaining ingredients in a bowl. Whip with a wire whisk until smooth and creamy. Chill until serving time (at least three hours). Just before serving, toss salad and serve in a wooden bowl.

Note: Dressing may be prepared up to five days in advance.

Preparation time: 30 minutes
Chilling time: 3 hours or longer

BARBECUED BABY BOAR

12+ servings

Hunting wild boar was risky business, especially because you got only one shot from a muzzle-loaded rifle. If you missed, you risked having an angry boar come charging at you! Of course, for crack-shot frontiersmen like Davy Crockett, roast boar was a common feast.

This mock baby boar resembles a roast pig at a luau. It's a big banquet, even for twelve hungry kids, since it takes a lot of meat to mold a boar. Leftovers make marvelous meat-loaf sandwiches.

Ingredients

4 eggs, lightly beaten
1½ cups apple cider
3 cups cornflakes, crushed
1 tbs. Worcestershire sauce
1 tbs. onion powder
1 tsp. garlic powder
2 tsp. celery salt
2 tsp. poultry seasoning
2 lbs. ground ham or pork
3 lbs. ground veal or turkey
2 pimento-stuffed olives
1 baking potato
2 parsnips, peeled
1 crabapple, or small spiced apple with stem
¼ cup apple jelly
Boar Barbecue Sauce (recipe follows)

Directions

Combine eggs, cider, cereal, and seasonings in a very large mixing bowl. Mix until blended and mushy. Break up meat, and stir into cereal mixture with a large spoon until thoroughly combined.

Line a large roasting pan with heavy-duty foil. Place meat mixture on foil and mold into a piglike shape (fig. 1). Press olives into the head for eyes. Peel a thick slice of skin from each side of the potato and cut into ear shapes. Press the ears into each side of the head. Poke holes in the snout for nostrils. Carefully tuck an apple under the snout as if it were in the pig's mouth. Cut parsnips about 6″ from the tip for tusks (pare down, if necessary, for a narrower proportion). Insert tusks alongside the cheeks (fig. 2).

Preheat oven to 375°F. Bake boar for about one and one-half hours. Draw off the accumulated fat with a bulb baster regularly while roasting. Remove from oven and allow to cool for about thirty minutes before trying to transfer from pan. Gently lift the boar from the pan using two wide metal pancake turners. If the foil sticks, lift it along with the meat, and tear it away after it has been placed on the serving platter.

Note: At this point, the boar may be covered with plastic wrap and refrigerated overnight.

Just before serving, heat apple jelly until melted. Brush the jelly all over the boar to glaze. Place parsley around boar as garnish, and serve barbecue sauce on the side.

Boar Barbecue Sauce

Ingredients
1 12-oz. bottle chili sauce
1 8-oz. can tomato sauce
½ cup apple cider
1 tsp. Worcestershire sauce
1 tsp. liquid hickory smoke flavor
2 tbs. red wine vinegar
¼ cup brown sugar
¼ cup molasses or maple syrup
1 bay leaf

Directions
Bring the ingredients to a boil in a saucepan. Simmer uncovered for twenty to thirty minutes or until slightly reduced.

Preparation time for boar: 45 minutes
Baking time for boar: 1½ hours
Preparation time for sauce: 30 to 40 minutes

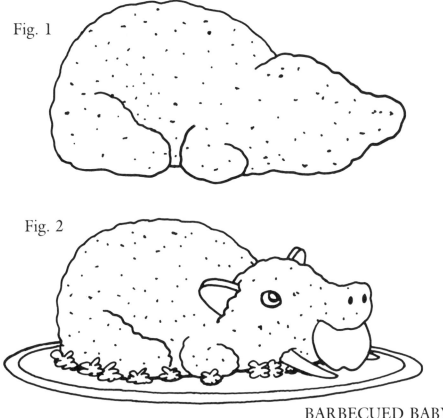

Fig. 1

Fig. 2

BARBECUED BABY BOAR

T O M A H A W K   P O T A T O E S

12 servings

Davy Crockett was a friend to the Indian people. When the Creek Indians were engaged in a battle against the United States Army, Davy stepped in and restored the peace. Both sides put away their firearms, and the Indian men also laid down their tomahawks.

Ingredients
12 baking potatoes
12 large pretzel rods or bread sticks
3 tbs. butter or margarine
paprika, to taste
salt, to taste

Directions
Cut sides lengthwise from each potato (fig. 1). Potatoes should be about 1½″ thick and flat on both sides, like a tomahawk stone. With an apple corer, cut a hole from the skin side of each potato through to the other side (fig. 2). Melt butter in a 10″ × 15″ jelly-roll pan. Place potato slices in the pan, then turn over to butter the top side. Sprinkle potatoes with salt and paprika. Preheat oven to 400°F. Bake potatoes for thirty minutes. Carefully turn potatoes, and sprinkle again with salt and paprika. Bake for another thirty minutes. Remove the potatoes from the pan and *gently* push pretzel rods through the holes (trying not to break the sides of the potatoes). Pretzels should look like tomahawk handles (fig. 3). However, never pick up the potatoes by the pretzels. They might break. Serve warm.

  Note: Cut, prebaked potato slices may be stored in the refrigerator overnight, wrapped in plastic. This dish cannot be reheated (the pretzels can burn).

Preparation time: 25 minutes
Baking time: 1 hour

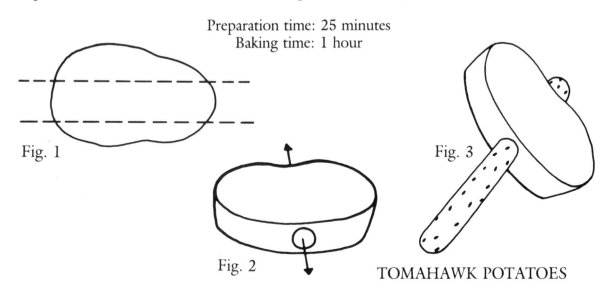

Fig. 1

Fig. 2

Fig. 3

TOMAHAWK POTATOES

B E A R P A W B I S C U I T S

(with Honey Butter)

20 to 24 biscuits

Legend has it that Davy Crockett caught his first bear at the age of three. Forever after that day, it was said that bears simply threw their paws up in the air and surrendered to Davy!

Ingredients
2 cans (10 count) or 3 cans (8 count) extralarge refrigerated biscuits
8 doz. whole blanched almonds
Honey Butter (recipe follows)

Directions
Open biscuit cans and separate biscuits. Stretch slightly into ovals and cut four slashes for toes (fig. 1). Place biscuits on ungreased baking sheets about 2″ apart, spreading toes. Insert the rounded end of an almond into the end of each toe. The pointed end will look like a claw (fig. 2). Be sure that almonds are pushed halfway into dough or they might pop out during baking. Preheat oven to 400°F and bake for about twelve minutes or until golden. Serve warm with Honey Butter.

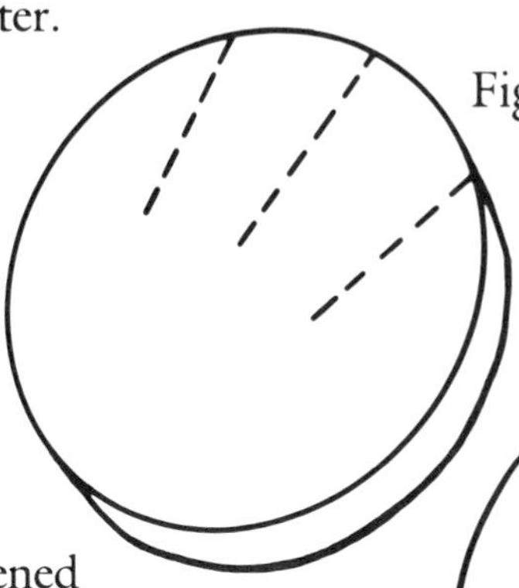

BEAR PAW BISCUITS

Fig. 1

Fig. 2

Honey Butter

Ingredients
1 cup unsalted butter (or margarine), softened
⅓ cup honey
¼ tsp. cinnamon
⅛ tsp. nutmeg

Directions
Cream butter until light and fluffy. Slowly blend in honey and spices, beating until smooth. Chill in refrigerator until serving time.

   Note: Biscuits are best prepared fresh on the day of the party. However, Honey Butter may be made up to a week in advance.

Preparation time: 20 minutes
Baking time: 12 minutes

DAVY CROCKETT'S COCOA LOG CABIN CAKE

Ingredients

2 cups flour
2 cups sugar
1 tsp. baking soda
½ tsp. salt
1 cup butter or margarine
1 cup flat root beer (or water)
⅓ cup cocoa
2 eggs
½ cup buttermilk
1½ tsp. vanilla extract
Cocoa Butter Frosting (recipe follows)
1 1.55-oz. milk chocolate bar (12 segments)
green gumdrop leaves
chocolate roll candy
whole cinnamon sticks
Tinted Coconut (instructions follow)

Directions

Combine flour, sugar, baking soda, and salt in a large mixing bowl. In a small saucepan, bring butter, root beer, and cocoa to a boil. Remove from heat and pour over dry ingredients in bowl. Beat until just combined. Add eggs, buttermilk, and vanilla. Beat with an electric mixer on low speed for one minute. (Batter will be thin.) Pour batter into a 9″ × 13″ cake pan that has been lined with baking parchment. Bake thirty to thirty-five minutes or until a toothpick inserted in the center comes out clean. Cool completely and invert from pan (peel away paper).

Cover an 18″ × 18″ board with foil to serve as a cake platter. Prepare frosting as directed and cut cake according to diagram in figure 1. Measure 5″ along length of cake, then cut crosswise. Cut diagonally across remaining cake square. Spread a ½″ layer of frosting on base. Sandwich roof triangles back to back with frosting. Set roof on top of base (fig. 2). Fill pastry bag fitted with #5 large round writing tip with two-thirds of remaining frosting. Pipe logs horizontally across front, back, and sides of cake (fig. 3). Fill another bag, fitted with #48 ribbon tip, and pipe shingles on roof. Cut a door out of the chocolate bar, using three connecting sections, and press in front of cabin. Cut apart remaining sections and use for windows. Press some gumdrop leaves around the cabin for bushes. Stack a pile of cinnamon sticks for logs at the back or the side of the cabin. Break chocolate roll candy in half and insert in roof (side by side) for a stove-pipe chimney. Spread coconut around cabin for grass (fig. 4).

Note: Cake may be prepared in advance and frozen for up to three weeks. Cover with plastic wrap after 1 hour in freezer.

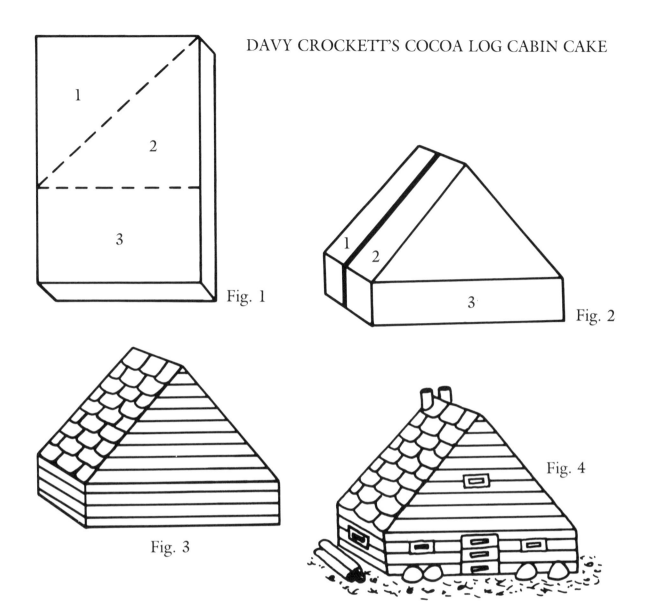

DAVY CROCKETT'S COCOA LOG CABIN CAKE

Fig. 1

Fig. 2

Fig. 3

Fig. 4

Cocoa Butter Frosting

Ingredients
6 cups confectioners' sugar
⅔ cup cocoa
⅔ cup butter or margarine, softened
1 tbs. vanilla extract
6 tbs. milk

Directions
Combine ingredients in a large bowl. Beat with an electric mixer until smooth and of spreading consistency, adding additional milk if necessary.

Tinted Coconut

Ingredients
2 cups shredded coconut
1 tbs. water
green gel food coloring

Directions
Place a drop or two of green gel food coloring in 1 tbs. of water. Add to a one-quart jar filled with 2 cups of shredded coconut. Shake vigorously until coconut is evenly tinted.

Preparation time: 1¼ hour
Baking time: 30 to 35 minutes

I C E - C R E A M   R A C C O O N S

12 servings

Ingredients
½ gal. chocolate (or coffee) ice cream
24 miniature marshmallows
24 chocolate-covered miniature mints or chocolate-covered almonds
1 cup fudge sauce (any brand that becomes thickened and firm when frozen)

Directions
Place twelve large scoops of ice cream (evenly spaced) on a foil-lined cookie sheet. Top each scoop with a miniscoop (fig. 1). If you don't have a miniature ice-cream scoop (½-oz.), try using a melon baller. For each raccoon insert two marshmallows for eyes, pushing down into the ice cream. Insert two mints or almonds at each side of the head for ears (fig. 2). Fill a small pastry bag, fitted with a #3 or #4 round writing tip, with fudge sauce. Pipe nose on small scoop. Pipe around marshmallows to form a mask, and pipe pupils on marshmallows for eyes (fig. 3). Return to freezer for at least three hours before serving.
   Note: These can be made up to a week in advance if you place them in a covered container or cover firmly frozen raccoons with plastic wrap.

Preparation time: 25 minutes
Freezing time: 3 hours or longer

128

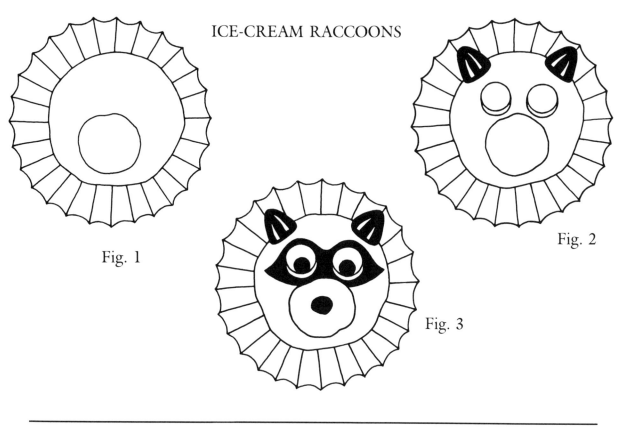

ICE-CREAM RACCOONS

Fig. 1

Fig. 2

Fig. 3

GEORGIE'S GINGER MOUNTAIN BREW

12+ servings

Georgie Russel was Davy Crockett's best friend and a fellow whose boasting frequently landed Davy in hot water! After a brush with danger, a cool refresher is always a welcome way to relax.

Ingredients
1 gal. apple cider or apple juice
1 2-liter bottle ginger ale, chilled

Directions
Fill about four ice cube trays with apple cider. Freeze at least five hours or until firm. Divide ice among the cups or mugs. Fill one-third of the way up with remaining cider. Fill the rest of each glass with ginger ale.

Preparation time: 10 minutes
Freezing time for ice: 5 hours or longer

BEAUTY AND THE BEAST PARTY

Ages 8 to 12

An enchantress turns a rude prince into a beast, and his servants into animated household objects. For the spell to be broken, the Beast must learn to love another person and win that person's love in return. In a nearby village lives Belle, a strong-willed young girl with a passion for books and a desire for adventure. One day, her beloved father becomes the unwitting captive of the Beast in his castle, and Belle bravely offers her own freedom in exchange for that of her father. An unlikely love begins to unfold between Belle and the Beast. Their relationship, once based on captivity, gives way to one of mutual respect, caring—and finally, love.

Invitation: Cogsworth's Clock Face

Decorations: French-countryside Motif—lace tablecloth; books; geraniums; candelabra; animated plates and flatware

Get-acquainted Activity: The Magic Mirror

Fantasy Feature: French Feather Dusters

Games: Dust Bunny Derby; Candelabra Walk; Once upon a Time

Menu: Enchanted Rose Salad (with Country French Dressing); Cheese Soufflé; Beastly Baked Potatoes (with Country Herb-cheese Butter); Belle's Beans Almondine; Candlestick Rolls; Chocolate Chocolate-chip Ice-cream Château; Mrs. Potts's and Chip's English Tea Cake; Chip's Cherry Tea

Cogsworth's Clock Face

With the hands on his face, Cogsworth the clock tells children what time to "be our guest."

Materials
12 8″ brown paper party plates
24 8½″ × 11″ sheets white paper
black felt-tip marker
stapler
12 9″ × 12″ white envelopes

Directions
Cut out twenty-four 6″ circles from the white paper. On twelve of the white circles, draw Cogsworth's face, making the hands point to the time of the party (fig. 1). On the other twelve circles, write the following message:

Cogsworth says
it's time to
"Be our guest!"
Join Belle and (your child's name)
for a
Country French Feast
at
The Beast's Castle
(address, time, and date)
RSVP: (your phone number)

Place a circle with Cogsworth's face over a circle with the party message, and place both circles over the center of a plate. Staple them together at the top (fig. 2). Repeat this with each plate, and mail the invitations in oversize envelopes.

Preparation time: 1¼ hours

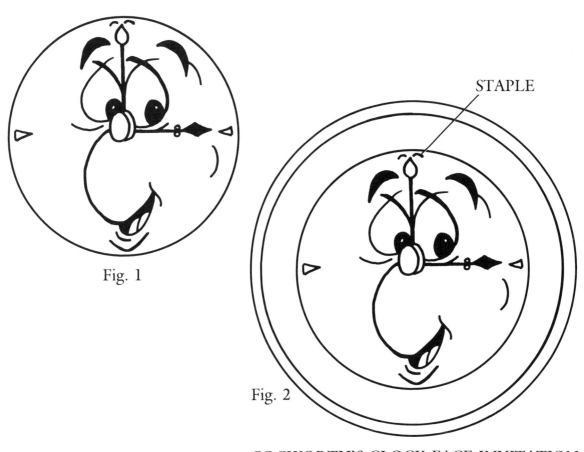

Fig. 1

STAPLE

Fig. 2

COGWORTH'S CLOCK FACE INVITATION

D E C O R A T I O N S

Belle's favorite room in the castle is the library, so over a paper lace tablecloth, stand several books up with bookends in the middle of the table. Try some clay pots filled with red geraniums for bookends to add to the French-country flavor. By all means, include a candelabra if you have one. Finally, "animate" the plates and flatware. If you're using plastic knives, forks, and spoons, cut 1″ circles from white or colored paper. Using double-stick tape, attach the circles to the fronts and backs of the flatware handles, and make faces on them with felt-tip markers. You can also draw faces on heavy-duty paper plates with nontoxic markers.

Note: Use permanent ink markers. Watercolor markers will smear when exposed to food moisture.

BEAUTY AND THE BEAST PARTY — Chocolate Chocolate-chip
Ice-cream Château (p. 142)

GET-ACQUAINTED ACTIVITY

The Magic Mirror

Cloistered in his lonely castle, the Beast's only window to the outside world is a magic mirror.

In this game, as guests arrive at the party, they gather around a full-length "magic" mirror and begin to play a game based on the same concept as charades. Out of a hat, children draw slips of paper that have been marked with the categories *who, what,* and *where.* Each player takes a turn drawing an image on the mirror, according to the chosen category. It can be a character, object, or place. The other children try to guess what it is. Provide watercolor felt-tip markers for drawing on the mirror, and have glass cleaner and a rag handy for between-picture cleanups.

FANTASY FEATURE

French Feather Dusters

The French feather duster makes a fun party favor. In addition, children get to use them in the Dust Bunny Derby game.

Materials
12 wooden paint-mixing sticks (from hardware or paint store)
4" colored feathers (about 2 doz. for each skirt)
¾"- or 1"-wide colored plastic tape
12 sets of plastic doll eyes with movable pupils (from craft or hobby shop)
2 feet ½" lace
12 colored tassels with 2" cord loops
acrylic paints
glue
scissors

Directions
An assembly-line setup is the best way to create these feather dusters, doing each step for each duster in turn, before moving on to the next step. First paint a hat on top of each stick handle (in the desired color, to coordinate or contrast with the feathered skirt). Glue the eyes below the hat and paint red lips and a necklace to match the hat (fig. 1). Allow the paint to dry. Flip the stick over and continue the hat and necklace on the back. Again, allow the paint to dry. Glue a strip of lace around the front and back of each hat brim. Loop a tassel through the hole in the hat (fig. 2). (If there are no holes in your sticks, drill them before painting.)

Begin taping feathers around the stick, starting 2″ from the base of the stick. Tape six feathers around the stick for the first layer (fig. 3). Tape six more feathers around the handle for the second layer. Continue winding the tape around the stick several more times (fig. 4).

Total preparation time: 1¾ hours
Drying time: 8 hours

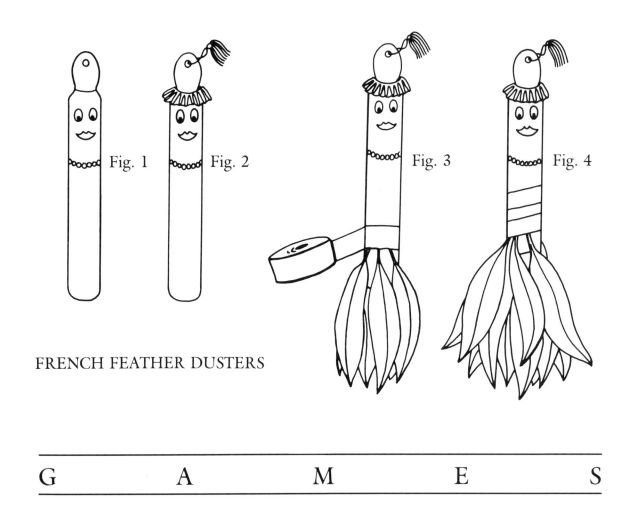

FRENCH FEATHER DUSTERS

Fig. 1   Fig. 2   Fig. 3   Fig. 4

G   A   M   E   S

Dust Bunny Derby

The Dust Bunny Derby is a race that works well on a long paved driveway. If you are playing indoors, add several laps to the race to make it more exciting. Use cotton balls or wads of lint from the lint trap in your clothes dryer for dust bunnies. Divide the children into three groups. (This makes it easier to keep track of which dust bunnies belong to which child.) Children in each group line up at the starting line. At the signal, the first four children sweep their dust bunnies, with their French Feather Dusters, in a race to the finish line. Then the next two groups of four take their turns. The winner from each participates in a championship race.

Candelabra Walk

In the Candelabra Walk, children take turns playing the suave candelabra, Lumiere, by balancing a cardboard candle on their head and hands. (Instructions for making the candles follow.) The object of the game is to time who can hold everything up the longest. One candle is placed on the child's head, and one is balanced on the palm of each hand. The child begins walking, back and forth, in a straight line. A scorekeeper with a stopwatch records how long each player can sustain the balancing act. The player with the highest score wins.

Materials
3 empty cardboard toilet paper rolls
6 gold foil doilies (8″ to 10″)
3 8½″ × 11″ sheets white paper
3 12″ squares yellow cellophane
scissors
tape

Directions
Place two doilies back to back so that the gold paper shows on the top and bottom. Cut an X in the center of the doilies about the width of the toilet paper tube (fig. 1). Push the tube through the slashes of the X so that the doilies line up evenly at the base (fig. 2). Tape the doily flaps securely around the tube. Cut a piece of white paper the length of the tube and wrap it around the tube like a white candle sleeve. Tape it in place. Pinch the cellophane in the center of a square and bring the ends together, forming a flame. Tape the flame down inside tube (fig. 3). Repeat all the steps with the remaining cellophane squares and doilies to make a total of three candles.

Preparation time: 30 minutes

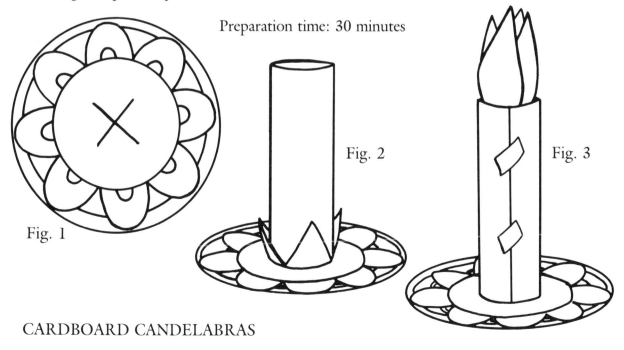

Fig. 1

Fig. 2

Fig. 3

CARDBOARD CANDELABRAS

Once upon a Time

Belle loves to read, and she marvels at the Beast's vast library. Here's a chance for party guests to write their own books for Belle!

In this group writing exercise, the end result is laughter, not literary greatness. Each author is issued a cardboard report cover filled with twelve blank pages (the number of pages should correspond to the number of children at the party). Each author makes up a title and begins on the first page with "Once upon a time," followed by the beginnings of a story. When the first page is full, each author passes the book to the author sitting next to him or her. That person continues the story on the next page. Pages three through twelve progress the same way. When the books have gone full circle, they will return to the original authors, who pen "The End" and sign their names. Afterward, the authors take turns reading their books aloud. Children love to giggle at the crazy composite creations, especially when they recognize their own passages.

Menu

E N C H A N T E D   R O S E   S A L A D

(with Country French Dressing)

12 servings

In *Beauty and the Beast,* the enchanted rose is a pivotal part of the plot. A tomato rose is easy to make, and when nestled in a bed of Boston lettuce, it becomes part of an enchanting salad.

Ingredients
12 ripe tomatoes, firm and unblemished
3 heads Boston lettuce
Country French Dressing (recipe follows)

Directions
With a sharp paring knife, peel the skin from each tomato. Start at the stem end, and continue peeling around in a continuous ¾"-wide strip. This circular strip is achieved by turning the tomato while you cut (fig. 1). Form a rose by rolling the strip in a tight coil (fig. 2). Prepare all of the tomatoes in this fashion the night before the party. Place the peels on a plate and cover them with plastic wrap. To serve the salads, wash lettuce and break it into attractive pieces. Arrange the lettuce on plates, and nest a tomato rose coil in the center of each plate, gently opening the coil up (fig. 3).

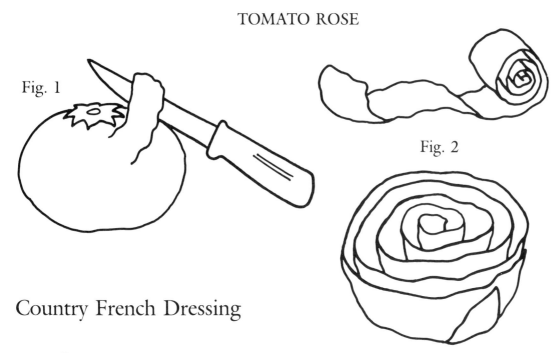

Fig. 1

Fig. 2

Country French Dressing

Fig. 3

Ingredients

1 tbs. Dijon or prepared mustard
1 tsp. Worcestershire sauce
1 tsp. celery salt
1 tbs. sugar
1 clove crushed garlic
½ tsp. chervil
½ tsp. dill
½ tsp. cracked pepper
¼ cup red wine vinegar
¼ cup lemon juice
1 cup vegetable oil
½ cup olive oil
2 tbs. fresh-snipped chives

Directions

In a mixing bowl, combine the mustard, Worcestershire sauce, celery salt, sugar, garlic, chervil, dill, pepper, and 1 tbs. of vinegar. Beat the mixture with a wire whisk until blended. Gradually whisk in the remaining vinegar and lemon juice. Combine the oils in one cup and slowly stir them into the bowl, pouring in a thin, steady stream. Fold in the chives. Chill the dressing at least eight hours before serving.

Note: Dressing may be prepared up to a week in advance and stored in a jar in the refrigerator. Shake well before serving.

Salad preparation time: 34 minutes
Dressing preparation time: 12 minutes
Dressing chilling time: 8 hours

C H E E S E   S O U F F L É

12 servings

When Belle has a feast at the Beast's castle, she is offered an array of delectable French dishes, including Cheese Soufflé.

The traditional cheese soufflé has one fatal flaw—it falls flat at the table. The soufflé in this recipe is much easier to prepare, and it doesn't fall flat. In fact, it's made a day ahead and allowed to stand in the refrigerator overnight (this is the secret to achieving a "soufflé" texture).

Ingredients
12 slices bread, day-old or slightly dry
2 cups Swiss cheese, grated
¾ cup cheddar (or American) cheese, grated
¼ cup Parmesan cheese, grated
6 eggs
3½ cups milk
1 tsp. dry mustard
1½ tsps. salt
3 scallions, minced
dash of pepper

Directions
Cut the bread into ½″ cubes. Layer the bottom of a 9″ × 13″ dish with the bread cubes and the cheeses. Beat the eggs until light and foamy. Blend in the milk, mustard, salt, scallions, and pepper. Pour the egg mixture over the bread and cheese. Cover the baking dish with plastic wrap, and refrigerate for eight hours or overnight. Bake in a preheated 325°F oven for one hour or until a knife inserted *halfway* between the center and the edge comes out clean. Let it stand for five minutes before serving.

Preparation time: 15 minutes
Baking time: 1 hour
Chilling time: 8 hours

B E A S T L Y   B A K E D   P O T A T O E S

(with Country Herb-cheese Butter)

12 servings

Here's a simple yet sophisticated dish that your child can help you make. Once baked, these warm potatoes are served with crocks of Herb-cheese Butter.

138

Ingredients

12 medium baking potatoes, washed and scrubbed
24 raisins
24 toothpicks (see note, page x)
2 to 4 dozen slivered almonds
2 tbs. butter or margarine, melted
Country Herb-cheese Butter (recipe follows)

Directions

Carve the surface of each potato as shown in figure 1. Cut the potato scraps into ear-shaped pieces and attach to both sides of each potato with toothpicks. Cut notches for the pupils and *firmly* press raisins into these cavities (fig. 2). (Be sure to pack raisins in, or they'll pop out while baking.) Cut two small notches for nostrils and cut a slice out below them for a mouth, inserting almond slivers for fanglike teeth (fig. 3). Preheat oven to 375°F. Lightly brush the potatoes with melted butter and arrange them in a shallow baking pan. Bake them for one hour or until tender. Serve them warm with crocks of Herb-cheese Butter at each end of the table.

Note: Baked potatoes do not keep well in the refrigerator, so it's best to prepare these the day of the party.

Fig. 1

Fig. 2

Fig. 3

Country Herb-cheese Butter

Ingredients

1 4-oz. pkg. herb-cheese spread
1 cup (2 sticks) unsalted butter
1 tbs. fresh chopped parsley
1 tbs. fresh-snipped chives
¼ tsp. cracked pepper

BEASTLY BAKED POTATOES

Directions

Allow the cheese spread and butter to soften at room temperature. Whip them together with a mixer until light and fluffy. Blend in the parsley, chives, and pepper. Divide the mixture among two or four crocks.

Note: This may be prepared as much as a week in advance and kept in the refrigerator.

Preparation time for potatoes: 35 minutes
Baking time for potatoes: 1 hour
Preparation time for butter: 10 minutes

BELLE'S BEANS ALMONDINE

12 servings

Delicate, thin *haricots verts* are expensive, difficult to find, and too extravagant for children's parties. You can achieve a similar effect with common green beans, sliced French style.

Ingredients

2 lbs. fresh green beans or 1 lb. each green beans and yellow wax beans
1 qt. water
½ tsp. salt
2 cubes chicken bouillon
3 to 4 tbs. butter or margarine, to taste
¾ cup slivered almonds
1 tsp. dried basil
salt and pepper, to taste

Directions

Remove the stems from the beans. Using a knife, slice the beans on a bias. In a large saucepan or kettle, bring the water, salt, and bouillon to a boil. Drop the beans in the water and cook uncovered for six to seven minutes. Remove them from the water and drain them in a colander. Meanwhile, melt the butter in a large skillet and sauté the almonds until golden brown. Then add the beans to the skillet and toss to coat them with buttered almonds. Season with basil, salt, and pepper while tossing.

Note: These reheat very well in the microwave and may be prepared up to two days in advance.

Preparation time: 30 minutes

C A N D L E S T I C K   R O L L S

12 servings

What a whimsical way to serve French rolls—as a candle holder for a bread-stick candle with a butter flame!

Ingredients
12 bread sticks or pretzel rods
1 cup (2 sticks) butter or margarine, softened
12 fresh French or club rolls

Directions
Arrange the bread sticks (parallel) about 1½" apart on a tray lined with plastic wrap. Fill a pastry bag fitted with a #5 star tip with butter. Starting about ¾" from the end of each bread stick, pipe a flame of butter. Do not use whipped or soft spreads; they are too soft to hold a shape. Place the bread sticks in the refrigerator for at least an hour so that the butter will be firm. Just before serving, poke a hole in the top crust of each roll. Carefully peel the bread sticks from the plastic so as not to break off the flames. Insert the base of each bread stick into the hole, pushing through the roll for a secure fit. Serve at once.

Preparation time: 15 minutes
Chilling time: 1 hour

CANDLESTICK ROLLS

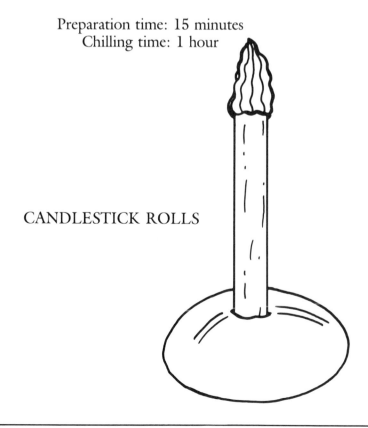

CHOCOLATE CHOCOLATE-CHIP
ICE-CREAM CHÂTEAU

12 servings

An ice-cream castle—or château, as a castle is called in France—is one of the great childhood fantasies. Now this dream can come true!

Ingredients

2 rectangular ½-gal. cartons chocolate chocolate-chip or chocolate cookies-and-cream ice cream (or your child's favorite flavor of frozen yogurt—this is lovely in raspberry), frozen very firm
1 1.55-oz. milk chocolate bar, broken into 12 segments
2 3½-oz. triangular-shaped chocolate bars
3 Chocolate-covered Flat-bottomed Ice-cream Cones (recipe follows)
Tinted Coconut (instructions follow)

Directions

The measurements of this structure will be approximately 7″ wide and 12″ high. Because you'll need to have some space surrounding the castle, plan on using a platter (or foil-covered board) that measures at least 10″ × 12″. If that seems like a tight fit for your freezer, you can always transfer the château to the serving platter at the last minute. If your freezer isn't tall enough, you can add the cones at the last minute.

Start by setting out all the necessary equipment and ingredients ahead of time, because you have to work *fast*. Have the chocolate bars at room temperature so that segments can be easily cut. From the 1.55-oz. bar, cut doors and smaller windows. Cut one triangle off one end of each triangular-shaped bar to shorten (fig. 1).

Unwrap one half-gallon block of ice cream and place it in the center of a cold platter so that it stands 6¾″ long, 5″ wide, and 3½″ high. Press the doors and windows into the ice cream on both the front and back. Place the triangular chocolate along the top edges to form the battlements (fig. 2). Use the second half-gallon to make towers, reserving any leftover ice cream to serve at the party. Place three scoops of ice cream on top, in a line down the middle, between the rows of triangular chocolate. Put another scoop of ice cream on top of the center scoop. Put chocolate-covered cones on top of each tower (fig. 3). Return the whole castle to the freezer at once. If you have plenty of space and ice cream, you can add one extra scoop of ice cream to each tower (fig. 4). Before serving, surround the château with green-tinted coconut grass or a blue-tinted coconut moat.

Note: The château may be prepared up to three days in advance. It must be frozen at least eight hours before serving.

CHOCOLATE CHOCOLATE-CHIP
ICE-CREAM CHÂTEAU

Fig. 1

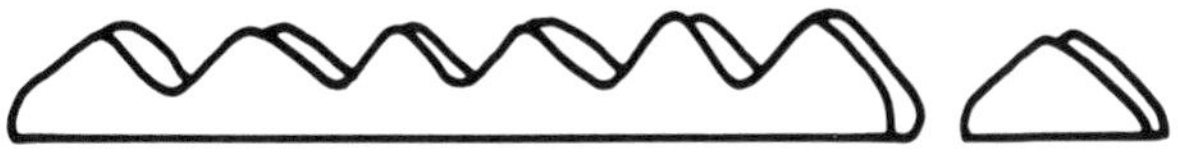

Fig. 2

Fig. 3

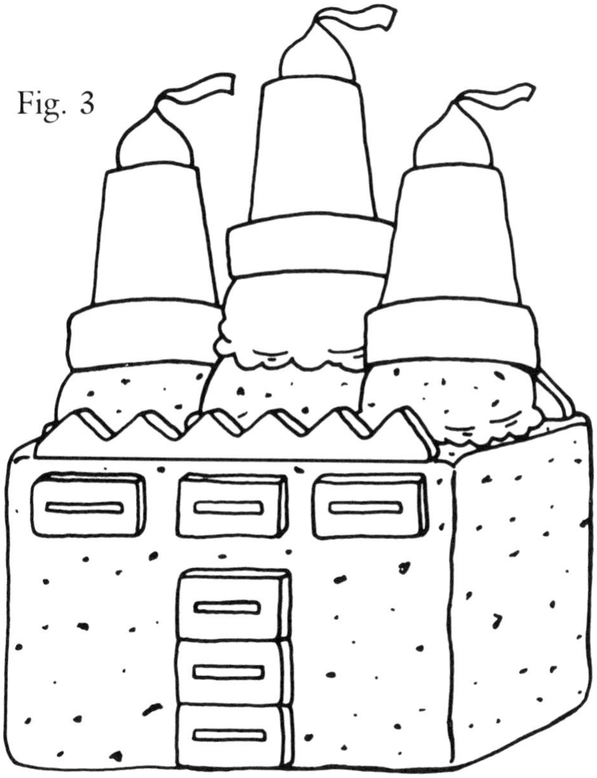

Fig. 4

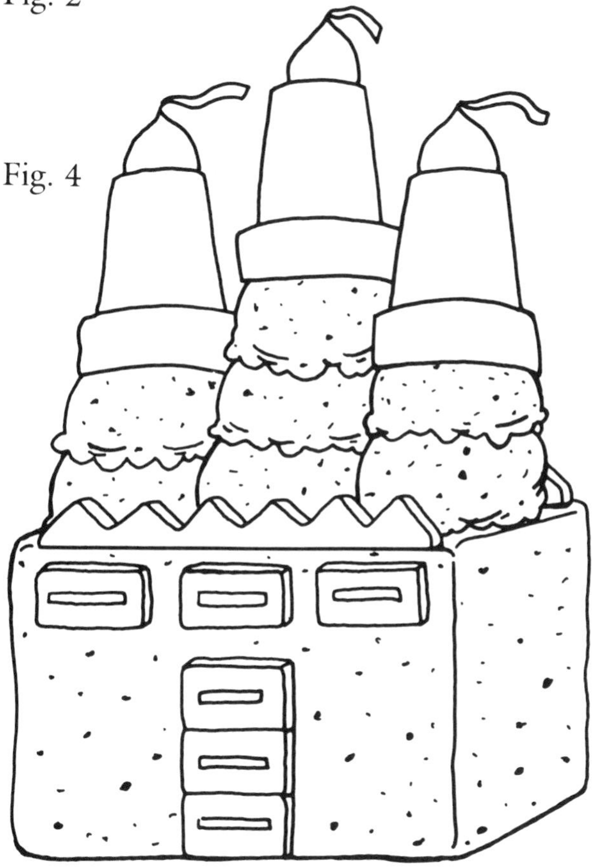

Chocolate-covered Flat-bottomed Ice-cream Cones

Ingredients
2 1.55-oz. milk chocolate bars
2 tsp. solid vegetable shortening
3 flat-bottomed ice-cream cones
3 gold-foil-wrapped chocolate candies

Directions

Break up the chocolate bars in a custard cup and add the shortening. Melt over low heat, stirring until smooth. (This works well with a hot plate or one or two minutes in the microwave.) Hold each cone over a dish and spread with chocolate. Allow excess chocolate to drip into the dish until the cone is completely coated. Invert each cone on foil. Gently press a gold-foil candy at the top of each cone, twisting the paper tail out so that it flies like a flag. Chill the cones to set the chocolate.

Tinted Coconut

Ingredients

2 to 3 cups shredded coconut
1 tbs. water
green or blue gel food coloring

Directions

Place a drop or two of gel food coloring in the tablespoon of water. Place the coconut in a one-quart jar and add the liquid mixture. Shake the jar vigorously until the coconut is evenly tinted.

Preparation time: 35 minutes
Freezing time: 8 hours or longer

MRS. POTTS'S AND CHIP'S ENGLISH TEA CAKE

12 servings

Orange pekoe tea is used in the batter of this cake, for a unique taste treat!

Ingredients

1 pkg. yellow cake mix
1⅓ cups strong orange pekoe tea, cooled
1 tbs. grated orange peel
⅓ cup oil
3 eggs
Orange Butter Frosting (recipe follows)
5 large red gumdrops
4 fruit rolls, apricot or banana
1 large marshmallow
2 miniature marshmallows
gel food coloring (blue, lavender, and black)

Directions

Combine the cake mix, tea, orange peel, oil, and eggs in a large mixing bowl. Blend the mixture on low speed with an electric mixer until moistened. Then beat at medium speed for two minutes. Pour the batter into two 9"-round baking pans that have been lined with baking parchment. Bake in a preheated 350°F oven for twenty-five to thirty minutes or until a toothpick inserted in the middle of the cake comes out clean. Cool the cakes completely and invert them from the pans. Peel the paper away from the back of the cakes.

Cut one cake according to figure 1. Cover a 14" × 16" board with foil. Arrange the parts as shown in figure 2. Prepare the frosting and smoothly cover the surface and sides of the cakes. Divide the remaining frosting into three equal parts. Tint one part blue, one part lavender, and one part black. Fill small disposable plastic pastry bags with the frostings. Cut ½" openings in the points of blue and lavender frosting bags. Cut a ⅛" hole in the point of the black frosting bag. Pipe a blue frosting band along the bottom of Mrs. Potts's hat (lid) and along the bottom of her and Chip's bases. Stretch the large marshmallow into an oval shape and press it into the teapot cake for the eye. Press small marshmallows into Chip for his eyes. Dot all the marshmallows with blue irises. Cover the top of Mrs. Potts's hat with lavender frosting. Pipe a scallop design of lavender along the blue bases on both the teapot and cup (fig. 3).

Slice three gumdrops in half and arrange them across the blue hatband to form a ruffle. Place a whole gumdrop on top of the hat. Slice about four ¼" strips of fruit roll and use them for gold edging along the gumdrop ruffle and along the tops and bottoms of the bases. Roll up a whole fruit roll and use it for the handle on Chip. Overlap two whole fruit rolls by about 1". Roll them up to form a handle for Mrs. Potts. Split the remaining gumdrop in half and pinch the pieces into mouth shapes for Mrs. Potts and Chip. Finally, outline the eyes with black, adding pupils, eyebrows, and lashes. Outline the mouths and (with lines) suggest cheeks and a chin (fig. 4).

Orange Butter Frosting

Ingredients
1 cup butter or margarine, softened
2 tsp. vanilla extract
2 lbs. confectioners' sugar
4 to 6 tbs. orange juice

Directions

Cream the butter and vanilla until light and fluffy. Beat in the sugar and enough orange juice until the consistency is smooth and spreadable.

Note: Cake and icing may be prepared up to three weeks in advance and frozen. Freeze for one hour uncovered, then cover with plastic wrap.

Total preparation time: 1½ hours
Baking time: 25 to 30 minutes

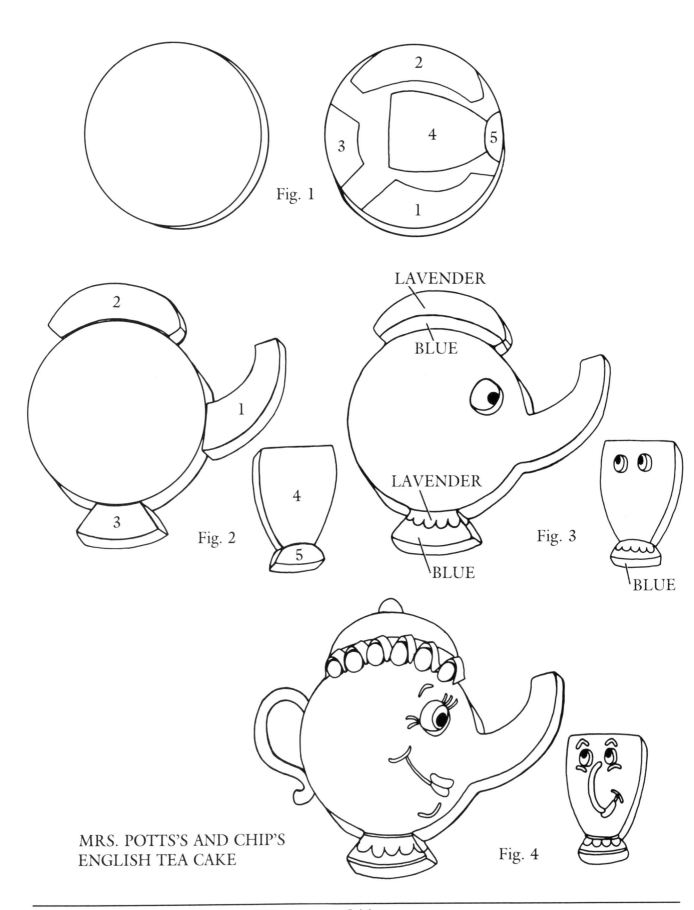

Fig. 1

Fig. 2

LAVENDER

BLUE

LAVENDER

BLUE

Fig. 3

BLUE

MRS. POTTS'S AND CHIP'S
ENGLISH TEA CAKE

Fig. 4

CHIP'S CHERRY TEA

12 servings

Most children prefer fruity iced tea to hot tea, but you can still serve it from a classic teapot.

Ingredients
1 gal. freshly brewed orange pekoe tea
1 cup Maraschino cherry juice (from jar)
½ cup grenadine syrup
2 tbs. lemon juice
48 Maraschino cherries, drained

Directions
Combine the tea, cherry juice, syrup, and lemon juice in a large pot (divide it into two parts, if necessary). Put a cherry in each cube section of four ice cube trays. Pour the tea into the trays and freeze them for five hours or longer. Meanwhile, chill the remaining tea. To serve, place the ice cubes in cups and pour the cold tea over the cubes.

Note: This may be prepared a week in advance.

Preparation time: 30 minutes
Freezing and chilling times: 5 hours or longer

SLEEPING BEAUTY PARTY

Ages 8 to 12

The evil fairy, Maleficent, places a spell on the newborn Princess Aurora, the film's title character: on her sixteenth birthday, she will prick her finger on the spindle of a spinning wheel and fall into a deathlike sleep. Three good fairies named Flora, Fauna, and Merryweather secret Aurora out of the castle and hide her in a cottage in the woods. They even bestow upon her a new name, Briar Rose. But on Briar Rose's sixteenth birthday, Maleficent's spell works its magic, and the princess falls into a deep sleep. Through the efforts of Prince Phillip, Maleficent, who has transformed herself into a terrifying dragon, is slain, and the spell is broken. Aurora is awakened by a kiss from the heroic Phillip.

Invitation: Castle Card

Decorations: Medieval Motif—brown wrapping-paper tapestries and banners; cardboard shields; foil swords; foil-covered throne

Get-acquainted Activity: Peanut Butter Popcorn Palace

Fantasy Feature: Magic Wands

Games: Scary Fairy Talethon; Spinning Yarns; Resting Royals

Supper Menu: Sleeping Beauty Subs; Slumber Party Salad Bar (with Dragon Dressing); Frozen Fairies; Woodcutter's Cottage Cake; Enchanted Hot Chocolate

Breakfast Menu: Aurora's Orange Toast; Cantaloupe Crowns; Princess Pink Pineapple Juice

SLEEPING BEAUTY PARTY—Sleeping Beauty Subs (p. 156)

Castle Card

A Sleeping Beauty slumber party calls for a castle invitation. The message is written behind the drawbridge.

Materials
12 sheets light blue construction paper
12 sheets beige or gray construction paper
tracing paper
pencil
white chalk
scissors
1 sheet thin poster board
black felt marker (fine tip)
brown felt marker (wide chisel tip)
paste or rubber cement
stapler
12 9″ × 12″ envelopes

Directions
On each sheet of the blue paper, smudge some chalk clouds around the top of the page (fig. 1). (These invitations are designed horizontally.) With tracing paper and pencil, trace the castle card pattern on page 150. Cut out the entire tracing and paste it to the thin poster board. Cut out a castle stencil from the poster board, and use it to cut out twelve castles from the beige paper. Cut out a section for the drawbridge (which will be reattached on the invitation), and draw stone walls onto the castles (fig. 2).

Draw wide boards on the drawbridge pieces, using the brown marker (fig. 3). Paste the castle onto the blue paper, and write the following message in each drawbridge opening:

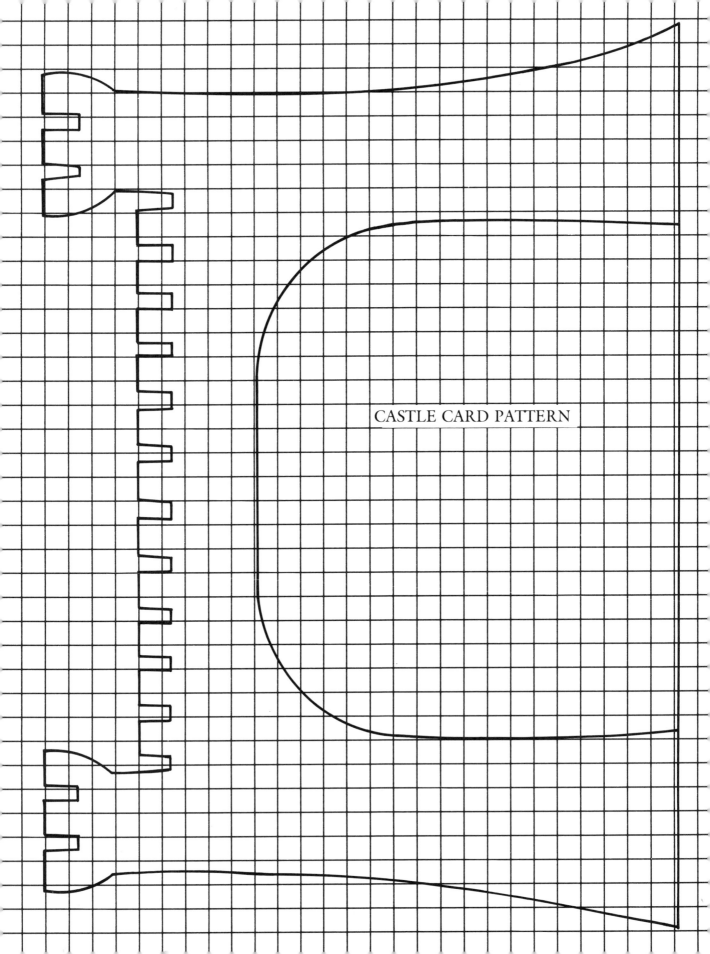

CASTLE CARD PATTERN

Come to (your child's name)'s Castle
for a
Sleeping Beauty Birthday Slumber Party
at (your address) on (date and time)
RSVP: (your phone number)

CASTLE CARD INVITATION

Fig. 1

Fig. 2

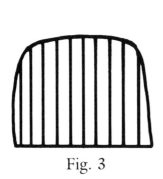

Fig. 3

Fig. 4

Staple the drawbridge over the message at the base of the castle (fig. 4). The drawbridge flap should pull down. Mail the invitations in large envelopes.

Preparation time: 1 hour

D E C O R A T I O N S

For a Sleeping Beauty slumber party, think medieval. Look for any decorations that might add this feeling to your home. Begin by drawing tapestries on brown wrapping paper. These renditions can be murallike scenes from the story. (If you're not much of an artist, don't worry.) Hang tapestries on the wall along with colorful cardboard shields and foil swords. A foil-covered chair makes a great throne. Medieval flags, also made from brown wrapping paper, are very dramatic when hung from the ceiling over the table. Paper plates and cups can be decorated with coats of arms (any design with castles, crowns, or lions). Finally, save room in the center of the table for the Peanut Butter Popcorn Palace.

G E T - A C Q U A I N T E D   A C T I V I T Y

Peanut Butter Popcorn Palace

Popcorn and slumber parties just seem to go together. Guests at this party gather in the kitchen to mold gooey globs of popcorn into a massive edible edifice that's fun to eat!

As the girls arrive, divide them up so that eventually there are three groups, of four girls each, mixing up the recipe. Everyone joins together to build the palace's foundation and create the towers.

Ingredients
3 cups smooth-style peanut butter
3 12-oz. pkgs. butterscotch morsels
30 cups of popcorn (about 2 gals.)
Chocolate-covered Flat-bottomed Ice-cream Cones (see page 143 and triple the recipe)
chocolate candies
4 to 6 1.55-oz. milk chocolate bars

Directions
For each batch, melt 1 cup of peanut butter with one package of butterscotch morsels in the top of a double boiler (or in a microwave). Stir the mixture until it's smooth, then pour it over a bowl filled with 10 cups of popcorn. Let the girls mix the popcorn and the mixture together until the popcorn is evenly coated. Cover a 20″ × 20″ piece of cardboard with foil. Begin the construction of the palace by using the first batch of popcorn as the base and the second and third batches as walls and towers. Top the towers with the Chocolate-covered Cones, and decorate the walls with chocolate candies for battlements. Pieces of the chocolate bars serve as doors, windows, and the drawbridge.

Remember, with this project, anything goes. It's creativity that counts. Once constructed, it may take several hours for the candy concrete to set. Use it first as a centerpiece for supper and later as a snack!

F A N T A S Y   F E A T U R E

Magic Wands

When the three good fairies Fauna, Flora, and Merryweather waved their magic wands, they sent sparks flying everywhere and caused quite a commotion. A magic wand makes a marvelous slumber party favor—for casting spells on sleeping friends or for waking them up with bouts of harmless head bonking! (Actually, it would be hard to hurt even a fly with a swat from one of these.)

Materials
1 pkg. rainbow polyester film
1 pkg. red polyester film
1 pkg. green polyester film
1 pkg. blue polyester film
1 pkg. gold polyester film
12 empty paper towel tubes
scissors
tape
curling ribbon (any metallic color that coordinates with one of the tissues)

Directions
For the streamers, remove all polyester film from the packages (except for the gold film), and keeping the film folded, cut through all thicknesses, at ¾" intervals (fig. 1). Unfold the strips into streamers and divide the colors evenly into twelve bunches. For each wand, gather the streamers at one end, and tape them down inside the opening at an end of an empty paper towel tube (fig. 2).

Cut twelve 6" × 20" strips of gold polyester film, and wrap them tightly around the cardboard tubes. Tape closed along the seams (fig. 3). Tie off the ends with the curling ribbon (fig. 4).

Preparation time: 1 hour

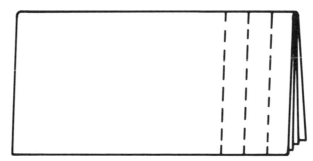

Fig. 1

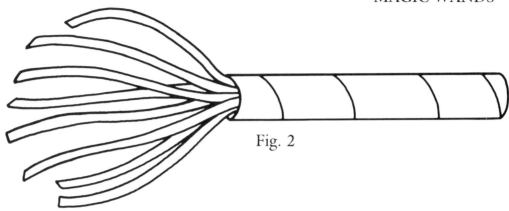

Fig. 2

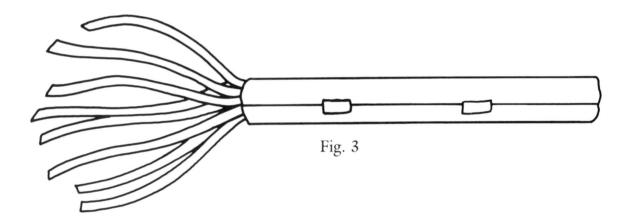

Fig. 3

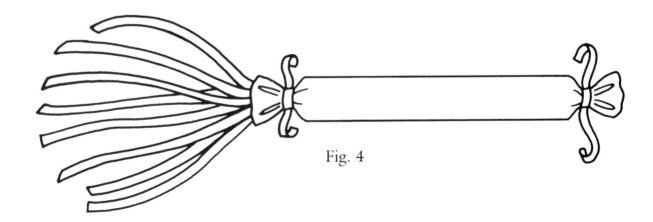

Fig. 4

Scary Fairy Talethon

Spooky stories and ghostly tales don't just happen on Halloween night—they're also part of the slumber party tradition. In this game, girls take turns weaving their own sagas of wicked witches, evil fairies, ferocious dragons, and dreadful dungeons. Everyone sits in a circle, the lights are dimmed, and a progressive story is begun. The sequence must start with "Once upon a time . . . and be followed by a two- or three-sentence contribution from each storyteller. As the story goes around the circle, there's only one rule to the game. Somehow it all has to end up "happily ever after!"

Spinning Yarns

Spinning wheels seem to pop up all the time in fairy tales, from *Rumpelstiltskin* to *Sleeping Beauty*.

In this game, the girls pretend to be princesses in a spinning race. The players are divided into six teams to see who can unravel and then rewind a skein of yarn the fastest. Each pair sits opposite each other about six feet apart. One player unwinds a skein of fairly fine gauge yarn in a continuous line to the other player, who quickly works to wrap the yarn around her hands. If the yarn snarls or snaps, it has to be straightened or tied back together before the players continue. The first team to finish is crowned "Queen."

Resting Royals

When Princess Aurora pricked her finger on the spinning wheel and fell into a deep sleep, the good fairies decided to cast the same spell over the rest of the kingdom. Aurora and the royal court slumbered away, frozen in time. It was up to Prince Phillip to awaken Aurora and bring the kingdom back to life.

This is essentially a shell game, using sleeping bags. One girl pretends to be Maleficent (the evil fairy) and leaves the room. The rest of the girls scramble about to hide deep inside someone else's sleeping bag. (For this scenario we're assuming that Maleficent would have wanted to foil the efforts of the good fairies and interrupt the sleeping court.) When Maleficent returns to the room, everyone pretends to snore. Maleficent walks from sleeping bag to sleeping bag, trying to guess who's underneath. She stops at each one and commands, for example: "Princess Hillary . . . wake up or die!" If it really is Hillary, she must wake up and come out of hiding. If it isn't Hillary, whoever it is "dies" (stops snoring). The last princess to die becomes Maleficent in the next round, when everyone switches sleeping bags again.

Supper Menu

SLEEPING BEAUTY SUBS

12 servings

These open-faced submarine sandwiches look as if Princess Aurora is sleeping on top.

Ingredients
6 7″ or 8″ hero, or grinder, rolls
½ cup mustard
2 doz. slices cheese (American, cheddar, or Swiss)
1 cup regular or nonfat mayonnaise
12 lettuce leaves, washed and dried (green leaf)
3 doz. slices (deli-sliced) ham or smoked turkey (extra thin)
3 8-oz. tubs soft cream cheese
1 can cheese spread (American or cheddar)
3 ripe olives, chopped into small pieces
pimento slices (just enough to slice into 12 tiny pieces)

Directions
Split the rolls in half lengthwise, and lay them out on your work surface, cut side up. Spread the rolls with mustard, and top each one with two slices of cheese. Spread mayonnaise over the cheese slices, and top them with lettuce. Fold twelve slices of ham into rectangular pillow shapes (fig. 1). Fold the remaining two dozen slices into fan shapes (fig. 2). For each Sleeping Beauty Sub, arrange two fan-shaped slices of ham and a rectangular slice to resemble a dress with a long skirt and a bodice (fig. 3). Fill a pastry bag, fitted with a #5 large round writing tip, with cream cheese. Pipe arms and a head on each figure. Pipe long golden hair with the cheese spread. Use two small pieces of olive for the eyes and use a small piece of pimento for the mouth (fig. 4).

Note: These are best prepared just before serving. You may even want to let the girls try making their own.

Preparation time: 30 minutes

Fig. 1

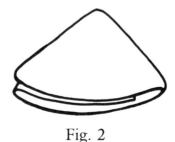

Fig. 2

Fig. 3

Fig. 4

SLEEPING BEAUTY SUBS

S L U M B E R   P A R T Y   S A L A D   B A R

(with Dragon Dressing)

12 servings

Spicy taco dressing warms up a salad like a breath of fresh dragon fire. Complemented by crunchy corn chips, it helps round out a sandwich supper. Set up a salad bar on a tea cart, and let the girls serve themselves.

Ingredients
4 heads romaine lettuce, rinsed and drained (shredded with knife)
2 doz. cherry tomatoes, split in half
4 bell peppers, chopped
2 15-oz. cans red kidney beans, drained
3 cups shredded cheddar (or Monterey Jack) cheese
8 cups corn chips
Dragon Dressing (recipe follows)

Directions
Arrange salad ingredients in separate bowls on a tea cart or table. Provide tongs and a ladle for dressing.

Dragon Dressing

Ingredients
2 8-oz. jars mild taco sauce
1 cup regular or nonfat mayonnaise
1 pt. regular or reduced- or nonfat sour cream
⅓ cup chopped scallions
½ tsp. seasoned salt

Directions
Combine the dressing ingredients in a mixing bowl, and blend with a wire whisk. Chill until serving time.

Note: Dressing may be prepared up to three days in advance. Produce preparation is best left to the day of the party in order to preserve freshness.

Preparation time: 30 minutes
Chilling time: 2 hours or longer

F R O Z E N   F A I R I E S

12 servings

Flora, Fauna, and Merryweather wear tall, distinctive medieval hats that look a lot like ice-cream cones!

Ingredients
12 flat-bottomed ice-cream cones (colored, if possible)
green, blue, and pink cellophane
1 qt. French vanilla ice cream
12 whole blanched almonds
3 ¾-oz. tubes cake decorating gel (one brown, one blue, one red)
1 10-oz. container frozen whipped topping, thawed

Directions

Prepare the hats first, before you remove the ice cream from the freezer. Poke a small hole in the bottom of each cone with a knife, and cut four 12"-square pieces from each color of cellophane. Pinch the squares of the cellophane in the center, and pull one through the bottom of each cone to form a veil (fig. 1). If you were able to find colored cones, use pink cellophane with red cones, green cellophane with green cones, and blue cellophane with chocolate cones.

Cover a baking sheet with foil and place twelve large round scoops of ice cream on it, evenly spaced. Push an almond with the pointed side up into the center of each scoop for a nose. Outline the eyes and eyebrows with brown gel. Color the eyes in with blue gel, and add a dot of brown gel for pupils. Pipe in the lips with red gel. Fill a pastry bag, fitted with a #5 star tip, with whipped topping, and pipe hair all around each head. Top each head of hair with a cone hat (fig. 2). Return to freezer until serving time.

Note: These fairies can be prepared up to three days in advance and stored in the freezer, covered with plastic wrap. However, this is another menu item that the girls might enjoy making themselves.

Preparation time: 20 minutes
Freezing time: Serve immediately or up to 3 days in advance

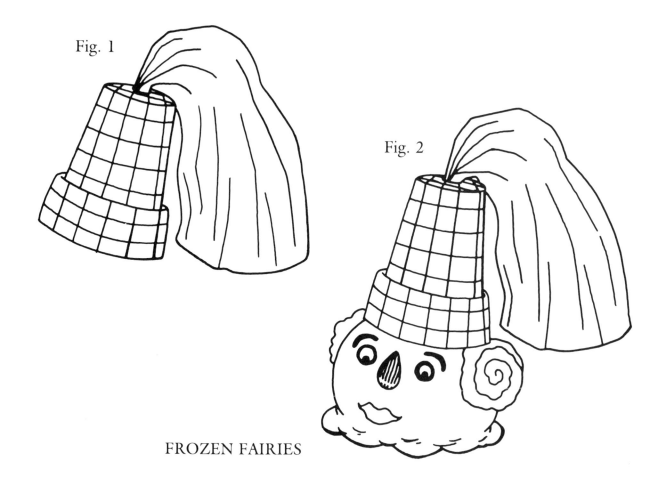

Fig. 1

Fig. 2

FROZEN FAIRIES

WOODCUTTER'S COTTAGE CAKE

12+ servings

When Maleficent cast her evil spell on the infant Aurora, the good fairies swept the princess away to the forest for safety. There she lived in a woodcutter's cottage.

This cake is similar to Davy Crockett's Cocoa Log Cabin. It has the same foundation, with just a little architectural renovation (such as its shredded wheat thatched roof).

Prepare Davy Crockett's Cocoa Log Cabin Cake (see p. 126) and cut and arrange per figures 1 and 2. Follow the frosting recipe for the log cabin cake, too, but reduce the cocoa to ¼ cup and the milk to 5 tbs. Then simply spread the frosting smoothly over the cake surface instead of piping logs.

You will need these additional ingredients: one box of large shredded wheat biscuits, eight to sixteen chocolate-covered pretzels (depending on the number of windows you put on the cake), four to eight sugar wafers, and jelly beans.

Split the large shredded wheat biscuits open and layer them, cut side down, onto the roof for a thatched look. Use chocolate-covered pretzels for shutters at the sides of windows. Place a sugar wafer under each window and top it with small jelly beans to resemble a window box filled with flowers (fig. 3).

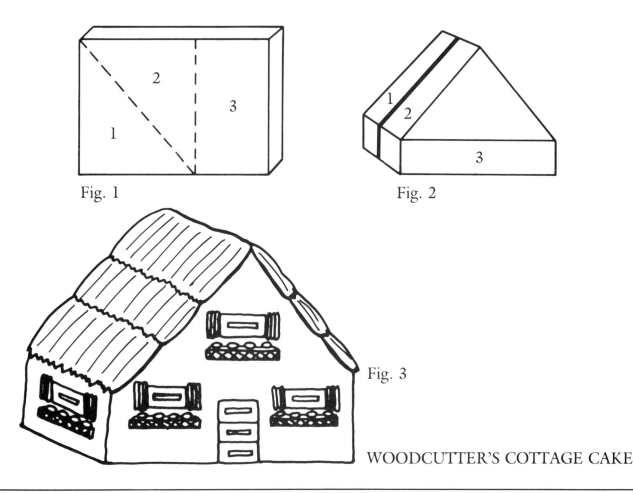

Fig. 1

Fig. 2

Fig. 3

WOODCUTTER'S COTTAGE CAKE

ENCHANTED HOT CHOCOLATE

12 servings

Hot cocoa spiced with cinnamon and apple makes a bracing witches' brew. It's even better when topped with marshmallows.

Ingredients
¾ cup unsweetened cocoa powder
¾ cup sugar
5 tsp. cinnamon
1 cup hot water
1 6-oz. can apple juice concentrate, thawed
3 qts. milk
miniature marshmallows
12 cinnamon sticks (optional)

Directions
Combine the cocoa and sugar in a very large pot on the stove. Stir in the cinnamon, water, and apple juice. Bring the mixture to a boil, and simmer for one minute. Blend in the milk, and heat through (but do not boil). Ladle cocoa into mugs, and top with marshmallows. Whole cinnamon sticks add extra flavor and can be used for stirring or as straws for slurping.

Preparation time: 12 minutes

Breakfast Menu

AURORA'S ORANGE TOAST

12+ servings

Simple cinnamon toast, spiced with orange, is an easy treat for sleeping beauties to fix the next morning, after they awaken. Make the orange sugar in advance, and set it out in shakers or bowls with spoons for sprinkling.

Ingredients
4 cups sugar
2 tbs. cinnamon
grated peel of one orange
2 1-lb. loaves of raisin bread
1½ to 2 cups butter or margarine, softened

Directions

Combine the sugar, cinnamon, and orange peel in food processor. Blend until the orange peel is very fine. Spoon into the sugar shakers or bowls. Let the girls toast their bread to desired darkness, then spread with butter and sprinkle with sugar.

Preparation time: 8 minutes

CANTALOUPE CROWNS

12 servings

Cantaloupe Crowns are a regal treat that can be made with grapefruit, if you prefer. (Do not peel grapefruit when making crowns.)

Ingredients

6 small ripe cantaloupes (or grapefruits)
2 pts. blueberries, strawberries, or raisins
3 boxes frilled party toothpicks (see note, page x)

Directions

Cut the cantaloupes in half using a zigzag slice (fig. 1). Trim a small slice off the bottom of each half so that it resembles a crown and rests flat on a plate (fig. 2). Peel the outer rind away from the melon. Let girls spear the blueberries, strawberries, or raisins with fancy toothpicks and decorate the points of their crowns with jewels (fig. 3).

Preparation time: 25 minutes

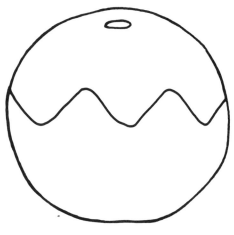

Fig. 1

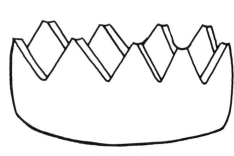

Fig. 2

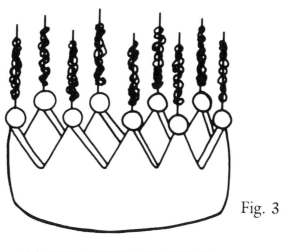

Fig. 3

CANTALOUPE CROWNS

PRINCESS PINK PINEAPPLE JUICE

12 servings

A touch of grenadine adds pizzazz to traditional pineapple juice.

Ingredients
½ gal. pineapple juice
½ cup grenadine syrup
12 small wedges of fresh pineapple (optional)

Directions
Combine the juice and the grenadine syrup. Chill overnight. Pour into glasses or paper cups. Cut a slash in each pineapple wedge, and serve on the edge of the glass.

Preparation time: 5 minutes
Chilling time: Overnight